T

TWAYNE'S MASTERWORK STUDIES

Robert Lecker, General Editor

THE MARBLE FAUN

Hawthorne's Transformations

EVAN CARTON

Twayne Publishers • New York
Maxwell Macmillan Canada • Toronto
Maxwell Macmillan International • New York Oxford Singapore Sydney

Twayne's Masterwork Studies No. 86

The Marble Faun: Hawthorne's Transformations
Evan Carton

Copyright © 1992 by Twayne Publishers.
All rights reserved. No part of this book may be reproduced or transmitted in any form or by any means, electronic or mechanical, including photocopying, recording, or by any information storage and retrieval system, without permission in writing from the Publisher.

<table>
<tr><td>Twayne Publishers
Macmillan Publishing Company
866 Third Avenue
New York, New York 10022</td><td>Maxwell Macmillan Canada, Inc.
1200 Eglinton Avenue East
Suite 200
Don Mills, Ontario M3C 3N1</td></tr>
</table>

Macmillan Publishing Company is part of the Maxwell Communication Group of Companies.

Library of Congress Cataloging-in-Publication Data

Carton, Evan.
    The Marble faun : Hawthorne's transformations / Evan Carton.
        p.   cm.—(Twayne's masterwork studies ; no. 86)
    Includes bibliographical references and index.
    ISBN 0-8057-9448-4—ISBN 0-8057-8569-8
    1. Hawthorne, Nathaniel, 1804–1864. Marble faun. I. Title.
II. Series.
PS1862.C37   1992
813'.3—dc20   91-34065
                                                                               CIP

The paper used in this publication meets the minimum requirements of American National Standard for Information Sciences—Permanence of Paper for Printed Library Materials. ANSI Z3948-1984. ∞™

10 9 8 7 6 5 4 3 2 1 (hc)

10 9 8 7 6 5 4 3 2 1 (pb)

Printed in the United States of America

CONTENTS

Nathaniel Hawthorne

Louisa Lander. Marble bust, 1858. Photograph courtesy of Concord Free Public Library

Note on the References and Acknowledgments

Several inexpensive paperback editions of *The Marble Faun* are usually in print, but I have chosen to use the standard *Centenary Edition of the Works of Nathaniel Hawthorne* in 20 volumes to date, William Charvat, Roy Harvey Pearce, and Claude M. Simpson, general editors (Columbus: Ohio State University Press, 1962–) for its accuracy and its general availability in reference libraries. All quotations from *The Marble Faun* refer to volume 4 of that edition. To place *The Marble Faun* in the context of Hawthorne's other writings, I often quote from earlier novels and tales and from his letters and notebooks. These quotes also refer to the *Centenary Edition,* which I abbreviate in the text as *CE,* placed in parentheses with the appropriate volume and page number. Quotations from *The Marble Faun* are identified by page number only.

The chronology of Hawthorne's life is taken, with minor changes and additions, from Nina Baym's 1986 volume, *The Scarlet Letter: A Reading,* in Twayne's Masterwork Studies series. I could not have significantly improved on Baym's fine chronology, and I am grateful to be able to use it. My selective critical bibliography obviously differs from Baym's, but in a few instances where the two overlap I have also made use of her brief descriptions of some studies of Hawthorne, especially her own. I also wish to thank Ms. Marcia Moss, the curator of the Concord Free Public Library, for providing me with the photograph of the marble bust of Hawthorne in Italy by Louisa Lander for my frontispiece.

The pleasure of composing this study was greatly enhanced by conversations about *The Marble Faun* with my friend and colleague

T. Walter Herbert, Jr. He and my student Kristie Hamilton read portions of the manuscript and, as they have done for me in the past, offered valuable responses. I thank them both. And, finally, I thank Janis Bergman-Carton, who has talked with me about the novel off and on for 15 years or so and has also sustained me in other ways.

CHRONOLOGY:
NATHANIEL HAWTHORNE'S LIFE AND WORKS

1801   On 2 August, in the seaport town of Salem, Massachusetts, Nathaniel Hathorne, Sr., from a seafaring family and a sea captain himself, marries Elizabeth Clarke Manning, one of nine children of Miriam Lord and Richard Manning, an up-and-coming merchant. The couple moves in with Hathorne's widowed mother and his two sisters. (Nathaniel Hawthorne, Jr., added the *w* to his family name when he began to publish.)

1802   Elizabeth Manning Hathorne, their first child, born 7 March while Nathaniel Hathorne is away at sea.

1804   Nathaniel born 4 July. His father is again away and does not return until October, remaining in Salem only briefly.

1808   A third child, Maria Louisa, born 9 January. Nathaniel Hathorne is at sea. In March Hathorne, Sr., dies of yellow fever in Surinam; in seven years of married life, he has been at home for a total of about seven months. In July Elizabeth Hathorne returns to live with her natal family, the Mannings, among whom her three children are to grow up.

1813   Grandfather Manning dies, and Uncle Richard Manning moves to Raymond, Maine, to manage family property there.

1813–1815   A foot injury is slow to mend, keeping Nathaniel from active play and friendships for about two years. During this time he develops a love for reading, especially storybooks.

1818   Elizabeth and her daughters move to Raymond. Nathaniel lives with them during the summers but returns to Salem during school terms. In Salem he is looked after by his Uncle Robert Manning, an energetic and successful man of business, a well-known horticulturist, and at times an overbearing guardian. Nathaniel misses the wilderness and freedom of Maine.

1821   Enters Bowdoin College in Brunswick, Maine. Much to his distress, his mother and sisters return to Salem.

1825	Graduates from college and returns to Salem. He has decided to be a writer and has bet his friend Jonathan Cilley a case of wine that he will not marry for at least 12 years while he devotes himself to his art.
1825–1837	Lives at home in Salem (his grandmother has died, and his uncles and aunts have died or moved out) and works on his writing. He reads widely in contemporary periodicals and New England history, which he uses as the basis for some of his most successful stories. Somewhat reclusive during this period, he sends his sister Elizabeth to the Salem Athenaeum to withdraw the books and magazines he wants to read.
1828	*Fanshawe: A Tale* (a short novel), is published anonymously. In later life he never mentions this work; only Elizabeth knows or remembers that he wrote it.
1830	Begins to publish tales and sketches anonymously in periodicals.
1836	Edits, with Elizabeth's help, *American Magazine of Useful and Entertaining Knowledge* in an attempt to establish a literary career.
1837	Writes, with Elizabeth's help, *Peter Parley's Universal History,* another attempt to support himself as a literary man. *Twice-Told Tales* (a selection from his previously published sketches and tales), is published under his own name. The book does not sell well, but it is widely and favorably reviewed. Elizabeth Palmer Peabody, a gregarious social reformer and fellow Salemite, seeks him out and begins to introduce him to people in her circle, including her younger sister Sophia.
1838	Becomes secretly engaged to Sophia Peabody. Begins to publish in a new political journal, *United States Magazine and Democratic Review.* (Most of his work published between 1838 and 1845 appears in this magazine.)
1839–1840	Financial security through literary projects having thus far failed him, Hawthorne accepts a political appointment, obtained through friends in the Democratic party, as measurer of salt and coal at the Boston customhouse.
1841	*Grandfather's Chair* (a children's history of New England from the Puritan settlement through the Revolution), which he wrote while working at the Boston customhouse, is published. Lives at the experimental Brook Farm community in West Roxbury, Massachusetts, from April to November, still hoping to find a way to support himself without giving up his literary goals. Discovers that, while sharing in the communal labors

and management of the farm, he is too exhausted and distracted to write.

1842   Marries Sophia Peabody 9 July. Moves to Concord, Massachusetts, where he lives at the Old Manse and comes to know major figures in the American Transcendental movement—Ralph Waldo Emerson, Henry David Thoreau, and Margaret Fuller, among others. A second and expanded edition of *Twice-Told Tales* is issued, as well as *Biographical Stories for Children*. He writes regularly for periodicals but is still unable to make a living as a writer.

1844   A daughter is born 3 March; Hawthorne names her Una after the heroine of Spenser's *The Faerie Queene*. Later in the year poverty forces the family to break up briefly: Sophia and Una go to her parents, who have moved to Boston; Nathaniel returns to his mother and sisters in Salem.

1846   A son, Julian, is born 22 June. *Mosses from an Old Manse* (collected sketches and tales) is published. In the autumn the family settles in Salem, where Hawthorne accepts a political appointment as surveyor in the customhouse.

1849   A new political administration dismisses Hawthorne from the customhouse in June. In July Hawthorne's mother dies. In September he begins to write *The Scarlet Letter*.

1850   Moves to Lenox, Massachusetts; meets and becomes friends with Herman Melville and has considerable influence on the writing of *Moby Dick* (which is published at the end of the year). In March *The Scarlet Letter* is published by the Boston firm of Ticknor, Reed & Fields. William Ticknor and James T. Fields become close friends, and their firm remains Hawthorne's American publisher for the rest of his life.

1851   Moves to West Newton, Massachusetts. A third and last child, Rose, is born 20 May. *The House of the Seven Gables* (a novel), *The Snow-Image and Other Twice-Told Tales* (a collection of stories and sketches), and *True Stories from History and Biography* (a second set of biographies of famous people for children) are published.

1852   Moves to the Wayside in Concord, Massachusetts. *The Blithedale Romance* (a novel) and *A Wonder-Book for Girls and Boys* (retellings of classical myths for children) are published, as well as his campaign biography of his college friend, Franklin Pierce, who is elected president of the United States. In July his sister Maria Louisa is drowned in a steamboat explosion.

1853   *Tanglewood Tales for Girls and Boys* (a second book of classical myths retold for children) is published. Appointed U.S. consul at Liverpool, England, by Pres. Franklin Pierce; has hopes of at last being financially secure.

1853–1857   Lives in England during consular service. Keeps extensive notebooks but finds it impossible to do any sustained and publishable writing.

1857–1859   Pierce is not reelected, and Hawthorne's term as consul ends. He lives in Rome and Florence and begins *The Marble Faun*, which will be his last novel, in 1858. Una becomes seriously ill with malaria and almost dies. Her illness lingers throughout Hawthorne's writing of *The Marble Faun*. The family is permanently affected by this near tragedy.

1859   When Una is well enough to travel, the family returns to England, where Hawthorne revises *The Marble Faun*.

1860   *Transformation* (the title of the British edition of *The Marble Faun*) is published 28 February. A week later the American edition, identical in all but title, is published. Hawthorne returns to the United States, and the Wayside, in June.

1860–1864   Tries unsuccessfully to write another long work of fiction, producing drafts and fragments of three different romances about Americans who seek to claim ancestral property in England. Also prepares and publishes essays on England drawn from notebook materials. His health begins to fail.

1862   "Chiefly about War Matters," a long article describing a trip to Washington and Virginia and offering reflections on the Civil War, is published in the *Atlantic Monthly*.

1863   *Our Old Home* (collection of his English essays) is published. He dedicates the book to Franklin Pierce, an unwise although loyal gesture in the midst of the war, when the Democratic party is much out of favor in the North.

1864   Dies 19 May away from home, while on a vacation with Franklin Pierce. Buried in Concord 23 May.

Literary and Historical Context

1

Historical Context

"That blue-eyed darling Nathaniel knew disagreeable things in his inner soul. He was careful to send them out in disguise."[1] So wrote D. H. Lawrence about Hawthorne in 1923. But his remark may be taken to identify a quality *in* Hawthorne, and to exemplify a response *to* Hawthorne, that readers have experienced in one form or another for 150 years. This quality of Hawthorne's fiction, and of the critical response to it, is one of doubleness, bipolarity, ambivalence. With respect to this quality, moreover, *The Marble Faun*, Hawthorne's last completed novel, is his most representative work. For while it has been much less celebrated and (after its initial popularity) less read than *The Scarlet Letter* (1850), *The Marble Faun* is the novel in which the forms of Hawthorne's own dividedness, and the opposing terms and concepts that give shape to his fiction, are most variously and vividly displayed. It is also the work that has elicited the most extreme and contradictory critical reactions and, perhaps, the most diverse interpretations.

The elements of Lawrence's Hawthorne—the serene, "blue-eyed" surface and the troubled depths of the disguised "inner soul"—are features in Hawthorne's tales and sketches of the 1830s and 1840s recognized by his earliest critics. Henry Wadsworth Longfellow, reviewing *Twice-Told Tales* (1837) in 1842, praised Hawthorne's ability to find "the picturesque, the romantic, and even the supernatural, in the every-day, commonplace life, that is constantly going on around us."[2] In Longfellow's estimation, Hawthorne was a good, perhaps the best, literary citizen of the young United States, a writer who took up and elevated American settings and themes to produce stories distinguished by their "unerring good taste . . . tranquil beauty . . . and healthiness of feeling" (Cohen, 12). In 1850, though, after reading the collection *Mosses from an Old Manse* (1846), Herman Melville dismissed Longfellow's image of Hawthorne and anticipated Lawrence when he described his Hawthorne, not as "a pleasant writer, with a pleasant style,—a sequestered, harmless, man," but as a writer "immeasurably deeper than the plummet of the mere critic," and as a man who "must often have smiled at [the world's] absurd misconception of him." In spite of "the Indian-summer sunlight on the hither side of Hawthorne's soul," Melville wrote, "the other side—like the dark half of a physical sphere—is shrouded in a blackness, ten times black" (Cohen, 32–33).

These early characterizations do more than offer alternative Hawthornes or establish the theme of a divided Hawthorne upon which later critics would play variations. They also reflect Longfellow's and Melville's differing assumptions about the vocation of the writer in mid-nineteenth-century America, and they suggest some of the tensions not just in Hawthorne's life and work but in his society. To a large extent, each of these literary contemporaries depicted Hawthorne as the kind of writer that he imagined or desired himself to be. Longfellow's Hawthorne is thoroughly socialized and civilized, a living proof that the United States could produce its own cultivated men—even men of genius—rather than turn to Europe for models. For Melville, Hawthorne is not a national representative but a secret rebel and nay-sayer. Thus, these two views of Hawthorne imply different visions of the social and cultural circumstances in which he wrote: the United States was seen in one instance as a noble and progressive nation and a rich subject for literary idealization; in the other, it was a complacent, self-deceiving, and perhaps even corrupt society to which the truth-telling writer stood in opposition.

What accounts for these alternative Americas? Is Lawrence's picture of a divided Hawthorne whose public expression disguises "disagreeable things in his inner soul" an apt image of the United States in Hawthorne's time as well? In many respects, it is. Despite the lofty sentiments of the Declaration of Independence, it had quickly become self-evident that, for all worldly intents and purposes, men were not created equal. The slavery system and the escalating controversy over its perpetuation and expansion provided the most dramatic example of social inequality in America. There were many others. American Indians continued to be displaced or slaughtered along the nation's advancing frontier. Recent European immigrants, especially Irish Catholics, were feared, discriminated against, and sometimes violently persecuted for their religious or cultural differences and for the economic and political threat that they posed to the preeminence of the established American Protestant community. Even for those who were not marked as outsiders by the dominant culture, equality and security were hardly the order of the day. The construction of the first railroads and the establishment of textile mills and factories in the decades preceding the Civil War had been the harbingers of a massive shift from a rural and agrarian to an urban and industrial economy. This shift toward a full-fledged industrial capitalism produced new economic opportunities and some great private fortunes, but it also widened, and made more visible, the gap between rich and poor. Laborers generally felt—indeed, *were*—more depersonalized and exploited under these developing conditions, and some began to think and speak of their lot in terms that linked them to the most disenfranchised Americans ("wage slavery," for instance). Women, whose equality was never contemplated in Jefferson's political rhetoric, had also begun by the mid-nineteenth century to think of themselves as an oppressed class and to define an organized feminist movement.

Racism, sexism, xenophobia, and class conflict, then, strained—if they did not explode—the myths of egalitarianism, classlessness, and the melting pot, myths already well established in Hawthorne's time and at least as old as J. Hector St. John de Crèvecoeur's 1782 essay "What Is an American?" These social divisions and inequalities in themselves, however, might not be expected to create inner conflict in white, male, middle-class northeasterners of old American stock, such as Longfellow, Melville, and Hawthorne were. But other cultural tensions, produced by the changing economic conditions and social values in the United States, strongly contributed to the unsettlement of the intellectual or literary class that was concentrated in this corner of the nation.

The militarism, expansionism, and populism of the 1830s and 1840s, exemplified by the figure and in the presidential administration of Andrew Jackson, had confirmed acquisitive and competitive individualism as the official creed of the American man. Yet the economic interdependency of people who increasingly lived in towns and cities rather than on farms, and the cycles of boom and bust that seemed to proceed beyond the understanding, let alone the control, of the individuals affected, posed disturbing challenges to this reigning ethos. Competitive individualism, and the geographical and social dislocation that accompanied it, also entailed a felt loss of community and connectedness. In the 1840s an array of communes, religious settlements, and utopian socialist collectives briefly flourished in response to this sense of loss. Hawthorne lived in one such collective, the Brook Farm community, for seven months. But for most Americans of the business and professional classes, the sole and sacred buffer against the law of the economic jungle was the family. Having no economic function either as a source of farm labor or as a site of staple production, the bourgeois family became valued for its very detachment from the marketplace; it was idealized, in the apt phrase of the social historian Christopher Lasch, as a "haven in a heartless world."[3]

To Hawthorne, the family life that commenced with his marriage at age 38 seemed both an escape from emotional and imaginative isolation and—although the needs of a family propelled him into business and politics—a refuge from all that was crass, compromising, or simply busy in the public sphere. He often thought of his wife Sophia as his angel of mercy, his personal savior, and, using a traditional image for the holy spirit, called her his "dove." Indeed, in the sentimental cult of domesticity to which the Hawthornes subscribed, the family became a kind of sacred object and a religious order presided over—in ritual if not in practical reality—by the "angel of the house." Of course, as feminist critics have shown, this worship of the middle-class madonna was one means by which a patriarchal culture prescribed and limited the acceptable roles for women and coerced women into measuring themselves by their performance in them. The sacralization of the roles of wife and mother also had a dark underside: not to be sacred was to be profane; not to be an angel was to risk being perceived as a demon.

That the family came to be viewed as an oasis of spiritual sustenance for a society principally devoted to material pursuits was due in part to the diminishment of the church's ability to fulfill that function. Especially in and around the cities of the northeast, the liberalized Christianity that had gradually replaced the rigorous and humbling doctrines of Calvinism could rarely convey a faith, purpose, or sense of community strong enough to stand up against the pressures and temptations of the marketplace culture. As Benjamin Franklin, the prophet and prototype of the self-made man, had written years before in his influential self-help manual, *The Way to Wealth* (1758): "In the Affairs of this World, Men are saved, not by Faith, but by the Want of it."[4] There could scarcely be a plainer statement of the antagonism between the ethos of competitive individualism and older notions of Christian fellowship and piety.

Hawthorne was not a pious man or a churchgoer, but, in a society that associated masculinity with practical concerns and material achievements, he was temperamentally inclined to speculation, imaginative life, dreamwork. And his speculations and imaginings were informed by his local and ancestral heritage, the Puritan sensibility—not transmitted as a doctrine but as a habit of thought and of feeling. Of his seventeenth-century ancestors, Puritan magistrates who had persecuted Quakers and condemned witches in their earnest attempts to combat the manifestations of original sin and the ongoing meddlings of the devil in human affairs, Hawthorne remarks in the preface to his first novel, *The Scarlet Letter*: "Strong traits of their nature have intertwined themselves with mine."[5] With such an inheritance, Hawthorne brought to his fiction, written in an outward-looking, future-oriented age, an intense and sometimes obsessive introspectiveness and a skeptical suspicion of the inescapability of the past. In a sense, Hawthorne spoke for and to the incompletely repressed Puritan consciousness of a society that, on the surface, was optimistic, individualistic, free, and unbounded in its potential for fortune and glory. For, as the Puritans knew, some of the vices that attend such worldly attitudes and ambitions are vanity, overreaching, self-deception, and the worship of false gods.

After his graduation from Bowdoin College, Hawthorne pursued his ambition to become a writer with nunlike devotion, living for 12 years with his cloistered mother and two retiring sisters in a house in Salem that he rarely left except for solitary nighttime walks. The willful isolation of this period, however, does not only reflect the single-mindedness with which he served his literary apprenticeship; it also suggests his uneasiness in his desired vocation, an uneasiness that no subsequent success would entirely dispel. Like other imaginative, intellectually inclined, and morally serious New Englanders of his class and generation, Hawthorne, as he entered adulthood, was faced with a crisis of social identity—a crisis that centered on the choice of a profession. In earlier times, a bookish young man of Hawthorne's background might have become a clergyman, but now the intellectual and moral challenges of the ministry seemed reduced along with the esteem and authority accorded a minister. Moreover, in a culture peculiarly obsessed with manliness—largely owing to the anxiety that the "sons of the Revolution" felt about their ability to live up to the example of the heroic "Founding Fathers"—ministers, and intellectuals in general, were often stereotyped as effete. As Emerson told the Harvard Phi Beta Kappa Society in 1837, several years after his resignation from his own Unitarian pulpit: "The so-called 'practical men' sneer at speculative men. . . . I have heard it said that the clergy . . . are addressed as women; that the rough, spontaneous conversation of men they do not hear, but only a mincing and diluted speech. They are often virtually disenfranchised."[6]

Authorship offered a speculative man another option and the possibility of recognition and social importance. Journalists and critics were eager to find and promote representatives of *American* artistic genius who might help the nation overcome its sense of cultural inferiority to England. At the same time, the audience for fiction was predominantly female, and increasingly the most popular and influential writers of magazine sketches, short stories, and novels were women—for whom writing was one of the only available public careers and means of self-support. For Hawthorne, then, a literary vocation bore ambivalent significance. It held out a social identity, and even the prospect of cultural centrality, yet there remained something frivolous and insubstantial about it, as Hawthorne's frequent term for his occupation—"scribbling"—implied. Fiction writing was work done at home, work largely done by and addressed to women, work that Hawthorne, especially early in his career, associated with resistance to or incapacity for "the regular business of life" (*CE,* 10:407).

Particular biographical circumstances, as well as general cultural ones, helped produce this attitude in Hawthorne. In his youth, the fatherless Hawthorne was placed under the care and tutelage of his uncle, Robert Manning, a successful, energetic, overbearing man. Reading and writing—which Hawthorne's sisters, living with their mother in Maine while he remained in Salem, could pursue at their leisure—were the ways in which he sought to escape the authority and the manly example of Uncle Robert. After becoming engaged to Sophia Peabody, and throughout the first decade of their married life, Hawthorne alternated between unsuccessful attempts to earn a living as a writer and working in the Boston and Salem customhouses in positions arranged for him by friends and admirers. Accepting necessity, Hawthorne nonetheless fancied, during the last and longest of these stretches of literary inactivity, that his own dormant qualities of rebelliousness and imagination were fully—and somewhat disturbingly—in evidence in the personality of his young daughter, Una. Una would be the model for little Pearl, the illegitimate child of Hester Prynne and Arthur Dimmesdale in *The Scarlet Letter,* and later she would have a more complex influence on the conception and composition of *The Marble Faun.*

When a new political administration withdrew his patronage job in the Salem customhouse in 1849, Hawthorne commenced his most productive period as a writer. Encouraged by an ambitious new publisher, James T. Fields, who hoped to capitalize not only on Hawthorne's reputation as a magazine writer but also on his recent notoriety as a result of the public debate that had accompanied his dismissal from the customhouse, Hawthorne completed three novels and two books of stories for children between 1850 and 1852. These writings won him fame but not fortune. The performance of a more mundane literary task, however, proved to be a significant step toward financial security. An old college friend, Franklin Pierce, was a presidential candidate in 1852 and asked Hawthorne to write his biography for the campaign. When Pierce won, Hawthorne was rewarded with an appointment to the plum diplomatic position of U.S. consul in Liverpool, England.

Hawthorne was almost 49 years old when, with his wife and three children, he set sail for Europe. He did not return home until the week he turned 56. In the latter years of his residence abroad, particularly after his consular service had ended, Hawthorne's characteristic sense of alienation and of uncertainty about his place in the world was as acute as it had been at any time since his marriage. He felt disconnected from the United States, writing from Rome to a friend: "I wish I were a little more patriotic; but to confess the truth, I had rather be a sojourner in any other country than return to my own" (*CE*, 18:140). In fact, before his voyage, Hawthorne's image of America essentially had been an image of his native New England, which he acknowledged was "quite as large a lump of earth as my heart can really take in" (*CE*, 18:8). By the late 1850s, though, as the country drifted toward civil war, it was impossible not to recognize that the United States was an ominously disunited federation of states, not a generally peaceful commonwealth, like Massachusetts only bigger. In his consular capacity as the overseer of maritime commerce with England, Hawthorne was also rudely awakened to the corruption and brutality that were rampant in the American merchant marine and to the apathy of the State Department and the Congress toward these conditions. But the long years away from home and the disenchantment of his provincial vision of America were not the only, or even the primary, sources of Hawthorne's alienation.

Hawthorne was a man who made sense of human experience by means of terms, concepts, and images that were deeply rooted in New England's history and Protestant culture. His moral and aesthetic sensibilities were formed by that environment. Europe bombarded him in his middle age with difference, otherness—not only different sights, sounds, and customs, but people whose lives suggested different orders of experience and different understandings of the workings of history and culture. In England he met Jews, including the lord mayor of London, of great importance and urbanity, while in Rome he encountered the poverty and, to him, sinister and doubly foreign atmosphere of the Jewish ghetto. Everywhere in Italy the art, history, rituals, and values of Catholicism confronted the New England Hawthornes; they exerted a powerful sensory and intellectual pull on Una and, unsettlingly, rekindled an old and theretofore theoretical fascination in Hawthorne himself. The principles of Hawthorne's identity were too firmly established to be radically altered by these challenging stimuli, but at the same time he was too observant, sensitive, and self-analytical to ignore or repress such challenges altogether. Meanwhile, as he extended his Italian sojourn from early 1858 to the middle of 1859, Hawthorne found himself once again in a kind of professional limbo. He was no longer a representative of his government, a man of affairs; but having written nothing in six years, neither was he a publishing author. He was not sure that he could complete another "romance," as he called his book-length fictions, and not sure that he still had an audience. *The Marble Faun* is a product of, and a response to, this imposing array of challenges and uncertainties.

2

The Importance of *The Marble Faun*

In the year of *The Marble Faun*'s publication, 1860, the union that had been established in 1787 by the U.S. Constitution was shattered. Upon Lincoln's election to the presidency, South Carolina seceded, other southern states soon followed, and in April 1861 the Civil War began. These were the culminating events in the breakdown of the early American republic, and they resulted in its disappearance. A different union was forcibly reconstituted by the victorious North in 1865: the war years initiated, for better or worse, the establishment of the country's mature, modern form. The events of these years *represented* America's transformation from innocence to experience, from unity to diversity, from a romantic or mythic self-conception to a more realistic and historical one—even if they did not themselves bring about such transformations, and even if national innocence and unity had never really existed in the first place. *The Marble Faun* is a valuable index to this transitional moment in American cultural consciousness. Published simultaneously in England under the title *Transformation*, Hawthorne's novel not only reflects its author's state of flux in the late 1850s, it also illustrates, in complex and indirect yet important ways, some of the larger transformations that were taking place in the United States—transformations in the nation's dominant attitudes and values, in its social composition, in its literary and artistic tastes, and in its international position.[1]

Like the Civil War in American history, *The Marble Faun* in Hawthorne's career has been associated both with maturation and with breakdown. F. O. Matthiessen, for instance, referred to the novel as "Hawthorne's maturely bitter fruit," while Rudolph von Abele saw it as a work of aesthetic and psychological "self-destruction," the final stage of "the death of the artist."[2] This latter view, often expressed more simply and moderately in the general opinion that the book is a "failure," has predominated for several reasons: because *The Marble Faun* is the longest, loosest, and murkiest of Hawthorne's four completed novels; because he could not finish the drafts for new novels that he worked on between its publication in 1860 and his death in 1864; and because of certain prevailing critical measures of success that will be examined in the next chapter. Negative evaluations of the novel, however, do not diminish its significance so much as they suggest another, and perhaps unexpected, kind of importance that it holds. *The Marble Faun*, as this study will show, poses a challenge to the very idea of a literary "masterwork" by forcing us to define what qualifies or disqualifies a work for that status and to examine the values that contribute to and the consequences that follow from our definition.

In other words, *The Marble Faun* is not a masterwork by virtue of the perfection of its form or the coherence of its thought. If it may be classed a masterwork at all, it is, paradoxically, by virtue of the suggestiveness of its breakdown. One of its most important suggestions is that every work of literature, no matter how inventive or original, relies on the systems of meaning and belief that govern human behavior and communication in the society in which it is produced. These systems or structures provide the terms and distinctions that are the writer's materials, the conceptual vocabulary that he or she manipulates in order to *make sense*. In its tensions and uncertainties, *The Marble Faun* offers us insights into the forms and effects of the breakdown of a culture's traditional systems of meaning and belief—systems that had given shape to religious, sexual, moral, and aesthetic life. These are insights that a less fractured work could not yield.

It is appropriate, given the kind of claim for its importance that I have been making here, that *The Marble Faun* is the only Hawthorne novel with a foreign setting; it is a book about Americans on unfamiliar ground. Many critics have judged the novel a failure either because of the supposed irrelevance of the Italian background to Hawthorne's moral and psychological themes or the inadequacy of Hawthorne's knowledge of Italy in comparison with his intimate understanding of New England. If we view *The Marble Faun* as a book about disorientation, a book about encountering "the Other" or "the alien," both within and outside of oneself, then these two objections to the Italian setting lose much of their force. In this latter view, Italy functions in part as a figure (and not, as we will see, an arbitrarily chosen one) for the state of metaphysical homelessness in which the American characters find themselves. In any event, *The Marble Faun* is significant as an early instance of what Henry James would make famous a generation later as "the international theme" in American writing. From James and Edith Wharton, through the post–World War I writings of John Dos Passos, F. Scott Fitzgerald, Ernest Hemingway, and Djuna Barnes, and on to the current barrage of novels and films about the Vietnam War, American encounters with foreign cultures have been a prominent subject of literary representation just as they have been a prominent object of political concern. These works, and many others, can show us how we interact with and define ourselves against others, and how we perceive or misperceive our country's role in the world.

Another common observation about *The Marble Faun* is that its genre is mixed or uncertain, that, as James wrote in 1879, "the book is positively neither of one category nor of another."[3] The two categories are romance and realism, between which Hawthorne's novel is seen to hang suspended, as it does between its Italian setting and its American sensibilities. In the prefaces to his previous works *The House of the Seven Gables* (1851) and *The Blithedale Romance* (1852), Hawthorne had characterized the romancer's art as a matter of "building a house, of materials long in use for constructing castles in the air" (*CE*, 2:3), of establishing "a theatre, a little removed from the highway of ordinary travel, where the creatures of his brain may play their phantasmagorical antics, without exposing them to too close a comparison with the actual events of real lives" (*CE*, 3:1). The phantasmagorical antics of *The Marble Faun*, however, are played out in actual and specifically identified streets, castles, churches, and museums, and the lives of Hawthorne's invented characters are constantly juxtaposed with references to real historical events and figures. Perhaps the best evidence of the novel's mixed genre is its initial reception: some readers took it as an allegory of the loss of Eden; others took it along with them as a travel guide to Rome.

In this particular doubleness, *The Marble Faun* may be recognized as a novel that prefigures, and in a sense embodies, the critical debate about the relative properties and merits of romance and realism in American fiction. This debate was vigorously pursued throughout the latter decades of the nineteenth century. It helped mold the imaginations and purposes of writers such as William Dean Howells, Mark Twain, and Henry James, as well as the responses of their readers. And, in altered form, it continues to rage today in discussions of the relationship of classic American literature to American social and political history and in arguments for and against the revision or revaluation of the American literary canon.

Finally, *The Marble Faun* offers its readers a unique opportunity to explore the relations between art and criticism, between the work of creation and the work of interpretation. It is a novel about artists who are constantly creating works of art themselves and analyzing works by others. In both cases, we see them struggling to make meaning; we see the complex interaction between the meanings they derive from the art that surrounds them in Rome and the meanings they invest in the art they produce. The very composition of Hawthorne's novel, in fact, exemplifies this interdependency of criticism and art. Many passages in which the narrator describes Rome or the characters interpret art were drawn directly from Hawthorne's travel notebooks; thus, *The Marble Faun* may be seen as a joint venture in which critical analysis and imaginative creation sustain and provide a context for one another.

In this respect, as with respect to the other grounds of the novel's importance that this chapter has surveyed, *The Marble Faun* is valuable for the questions it raises rather than for any neat resolution it achieves. If critical interpretation and imaginative creation are inseparable, can there be an "original" work of art that is not an interpretive variation on some preexisting model? Can there be a definitive or "true" interpretation that is not an imaginative projection of the interpreter? These are central and disturbing questions for artists and critics. Few works of literature or criticism, however, risk asking them as openly and insistently as does *The Marble Faun*.

3

Critical Transformations

Shortly after the appearance of *The Marble Faun*, Hawthorne wrote to his American publisher: "If I have written anything well, it should be this Romance; for I have never thought or felt more deeply, or taken more pains" (*CE*, 18:262). Several months earlier, though, as he revised the final chapters, his opinion had been more characteristically equivocal: "I . . . admire it exceedingly, at intervals," he confessed, "but am liable to cold fits, during which I think it the most infernal nonsense" (*CE*, 18:196). Hawthorne's anxiety about the book's reception is apparent in the preface that he composed, as he had done for each of his three previous novels. There, he worries that his "all-sympathizing critic" (*CE*, 4:1) may have moved and left no forwarding address, or even died, in the eight years that have passed since the publication of *The Blithedale Romance*. And he betrays some doubt about the new novel's suitability to American tastes and values when he explains that Italy afforded him a setting for his story (and a place in which to write it) "where actualities would not be so terribly insisted upon, as they are, and must needs be, in America" (3). There is even the suggestion of something corrupt or subversive about *The Marble Faun* in Hawthorne's fanciful remark that "romance and poetry, like ivy, lichens, and wall-flowers, need Ruin to make them grow" (3).

A new book by Nathaniel Hawthorne after so many years was something of an event in northeastern literary circles, and 14,500 sets of the two-volume American edition of *The Marble Faun* were sold before the end of 1860. These American figures, combined with the several thousand copies of *Transformation* sold in England, made *The Marble Faun* Hawthorne's biggest popular success. But critical response was mixed from the outset. Some friends, literary acquaintances, and longtime admirers wrote enthusiastic reviews in which they deemed the various aspects of the novel to be complementary rather than contradictory or simply disconnected. The poet and critic James Russell Lowell applauded Hawthorne's ability to enhance a "parable of the development of the Christian Idea" with "the most august truths of psychology" and with "criticisms of pictures and statues [that are] always delicate, often profound" (Cohen, 77–78). The influential reviewer Edwin Percy Whipple pronounced this "the greatest of [Hawthorne's] works" and marveled at "how closely accurate observation is connected with the highest powers of the intellect and imagination" (Cohen, 88). Yet even Whipple, so reliable an ally that Hawthorne had suggested a month before the novel's publication that he be asked to read the manuscript and decide on the best title, tempered his praise with the complaint that "this story begins in mystery only to end in mist," that "Hawthorne's logic of events leaves us in the end bewildered in a labyrinth of guesses" (Cohen, 89–90). Less sympathetic notices called the book "desolately incoherent," a "mere fermentation of impressions," a "romance run mad" (*CE*, 4:xxxiii). So widespread, in fact, were objections to the inconclusiveness of *The Marble Faun* that, within three weeks of its initial publication, Hawthorne had prepared a five-page explanatory postscript to be included in all subsequent printings.

In 1879 Henry James, who had settled in London three years before, published a study entitled simply *Hawthorne* in the Macmillan critical series *English Men of Letters*, edited by John Morley. Hawthorne was the sole American among the 39 featured writers, and

James, the sole American contributor to the series, duly confirmed its editor's implicit judgment that Hawthorne was the first, and only, writer of stature that the United States had produced. James reported that *The Marble Faun* had "probably become the most popular of Hawthorne's four novels. It is part of the intellectual equipment of the Anglo-Saxon visitor to Rome, and is read by every English-speaking traveller who arrives there, who has been there, or who expects to go." Despite the book's (somewhat exaggerated) popularity, James made it clear that he was "far from regarding it as the masterpiece of the author, a position to which we sometimes hear it assigned" (James, 131). Those who regarded *The Marble Faun* as Hawthorne's masterpiece surely comprised a minority party in 1879, but after James's study there would remain no such party at all.

To James, *The Marble Faun* confirmed Hawthorne's position as "the last of the old-fashioned Americans" (James, 128), a "beautiful, natural, original genius [whose] life had been singularly exempt from worldly preoccupations" (James, 144) and who therefore had no business writing about European cities and the history of art. His Italian novel contained some admirable details, James contended, but the whole thing was "less simple and complete" than the three tales of American life and suffered from Hawthorne's unwise attempt to "project himself into an atmosphere in which he [had] not a transmitted and inherited property" (James, 131). Only a more cosmopolitan American of a later generation who had immersed himself in European culture as a resident rather than a tourist—a writer, that is, like James himself—might hope to succeed with such material.

In the last decades of the nineteenth century, the United States pursued its "worldly preoccupation" with economic and political power on an international scale, and realism was the literary order of the day. Like any younger generation, the new realists defined their creative achievements and critical principles against what had come before. These writers (a number of whom had worked as news reporters) were influenced by the modern journalistic and photographic aesthetic of empiricism, immediacy, tonal objectivity, and social detail. They saw the fiction that had come before—however imaginative it had been—as idealizing, abstractly moralizing, insufficiently concerned with plausibility, and in short, lacking in rigor. The most critically celebrated practitioner of that earlier fiction, Nathaniel Hawthorne, had even had a name for it and had himself contrasted it with novels of "the actual" or, in the new generation's term, realism: that name was "romance." Hawthorne thus became for this generation not just a classic American writer but the classic romancer, and the mark of a romancer, as James put it, was that he depicts "experience disengaged, disembroiled, disencumbered, exempt from the conditions that we usually know to attach to it."[1] Hawthorne's tales and earlier novels accorded more closely with this conception of his work than did *The Marble Faun*. The ancestral curse in *The House of the Seven Gables*, the mesmeric visions of the veiled lady in *The Blithedale Romance*, and the famous scarlet *A* emblazoned in the night sky and in Arthur Dimmesdale's flesh seemed better representations of experience exempt from ordinary circumstances than did the wanderings of American artists through the dirty streets, the overloaded picture galleries, and the historical ruins of Rome. One reason for the critical demotion of Hawthorne's last novel in these years, then, was that it was least like "Hawthorne."

Another reason was Hawthorne's identification with America's colonial past and, specifically, with the effects of Puritanism on the nation's cultural development. Whether this Puritan legacy was honored or condemned, it was nonetheless seen as something essentially American at a time when "Americanness" was a more elusive and unstable quality than ever before. In the last years of the nineteenth century and the first years of the twentieth, immigrants—including southern and eastern Europeans and others distinctly "foreign" in behavior and appearance—entered the United States in unprecedented numbers. For cultural and political leaders, the articulation of established *American* traditions and the assimilation of the newcomers to them were urgent tasks on the national agenda. As "the last of the old-fashioned Americans," Hawthorne was a writer in whose work the country's heritage was preserved and communicated—but not, surely, in a novel set in foreign surroundings and featuring characters who shared the very ethnicities, Italian and Jewish, of many of the immigrants then in need of Americanization.

Hawthorne's general stature ensured that *The Marble Faun* would continue to be read and even to receive respectful critical attention, but well into this century it was commonly held to be a book marred by intrusive and unassimilated foreign materials, a book whose confusion registered its author's physical and imaginative distance from home. Hawthorne's uprootedness, argued Newton Arvin in his 1929 biography, was the cause of "much that is ambiguous and unsatisfactory in the book. For of all Hawthorne's finished romances it is at once the most ambitious and the least successful."[2] By 1948 Roy Harvey Pearce could begin his essay "Hawthorne and the Twilight of Romance" by remarking offhandedly that the judgment of *The Marble Faun*'s "inadequacy and failure ... has become virtually a commonplace in our criticism."[3] And Pearce eloquently endorsed this common wisdom: "Once received, integrated, localized, firmly grasped values and value patterns are lost, feeling takes the place of comprehending, grandiosity the place of grandeur, pathos the place of understanding, a *Marble Faun* the place of a *Scarlet Letter*" (Pearce 1969, 191).

The argument that *The Marble Faun* fails because of Hawthorne's cultural limitations or alienation from his true cultural element is a formalistic as well as an ideological one. Pearce's language suggests the formalistic dimension of this objection to the novel in its obvious preference for neat comprehension over messy feeling in a literary work and in its lament for Hawthorne's loss of the "firmly grasped," the "integrated," the "pattern[ed]." This line of modern criticism also begins with James, who, as we have seen, faulted *The Marble Faun* for being "less simple and complete" than Hawthorne's other romances. But formalistic analysis and evaluation of literature became a dominant and institutionalized critical practice only with the emergence in the 1940s and 1950s of what is now known as the New Criticism. A key tenet of the New Criticism was that a piece of writing attains the status of a work of art through its qualities of form rather than its subject matter, which cannot be particular to artistic representation. New Critics tended to value balanced, tightly structured, highly crafted literary forms; for this reason, many of the most influential New Critics concerned themselves almost exclusively with poems. In such a critical climate, *The Marble Faun* was found lacking on formal grounds. Wrote Mark Van Doren in 1949, "This story has no heart; its meaning is distributed, as its emphasis is vague."[4]

The New Criticism offered new criteria for success that *The Marble Faun* could not fulfill, but it also provided techniques for the discovery of new meanings in the novel and a vocabulary for reevaluating its importance. Their habit of detailed attention to the literary object sensitized the New Critics to the workings of the symbols and associated images that were embedded in the language of texts and could be organized to reveal unapparent patterns of significance. To recognize and understand these patterns, moreover, critics began to draw on the modern social sciences, such as anthropology and psychology, which suggested that the most profound structuring principles of any product of culture or the human mind might be those concealed below the surface. This ideal is reflected in the essay on *The Marble Faun* selected for the critical volume whose publication marked the centenary of Hawthorne's death. "At all events," Harry Levin concluded, "though *The Marble Faun* may not be as compact or controlled as Hawthorne's former successes, there are moments when it reaches farther or plunges deeper."[5]

The dramatic expansion of college and university education that followed the Second World War necessarily increased the ranks of professors of literature. For these teachers and scholars, intellectual esteem and career advancement depended upon the publication of original literary criticism. And since relatively neglected books by indisputably major writers were fertile ground for interpretive tillage, professional readers used their New Critical tools to bring forth readings from the farthest reaches and the most plunging depths of such works as *The Marble Faun*. Changing tastes and the new methods of and institutional pressures on literary criticism also enhanced the repute of Hawthorne's last novel. The work's notorious ambiguity began to look less like a sign of authorial incompetence and more like a prophetic insight into the modern condition. Some of *The Marble Faun*'s major themes—mysterious compulsion, emotional isolation, surveillance, incest, inescapable corruption—seemed to be the themes of modern life, the touchstones of what the critic Richard Chase termed "the dark center of the twentieth century" (Pearce 1964, 350). In this context, as Seymour L. Gross and Randall Stewart observed in their essay "The Hawthorne Revival," Hawthorne's writings about moral failure and the fall from innocence can be reconceived as figurative depictions of the political and psychological realities of human life (Pearce 1964, 356–57). Thus, "the last of the old-fashioned Americans" was transformed by some into the first of the moderns.

The multiplication of critical theories and methods in recent years has stimulated many new kinds of interest in *The Marble Faun* and has generated some perspectives on the novel that would not have been available to earlier readers. A work such as *The Marble Faun* particularly benefits from the emergence of such approaches as feminism, deconstruction, psychoanalytical criticism, and ideological analysis because these approaches are concerned not with its formal unity but with its relations to the social systems, sign systems, and complexes of desire and belief that surround and permeate it. One profound consequence of these new kinds of interest is that, for much contemporary criticism, fragmentation and discontinuity in a literary text do not obstruct or limit the text's meaningfulness but in fact are the keys to its meaning. These new keys, however, cannot be said to have unlocked the identity of *The Marble Faun;* or, more accurately, they have unlocked numerous critical entrances to the novel only to find a different *Marble Faun* behind each door.

A brief and partial survey of critical readings of the novel in the last dozen years alone reveals that *The Marble Faun* is a work in which art is ample recompense for the loss of Eden[6] and in which art is sacrificed to priggishness.[7] It is a "last attempt to affirm the upward course of American history"[8] and a radical attempt to challenge the complacent historical understanding of American readers[9]; a typological allegory of redemption[10] and a "contemporary fiction of surveillance, detection, and intrigue, set in the topography of an historical police state"[11]; a "marvellously realised debate about the nature of art"[12] and a catalogue of "empty banalities"[13]; a work of "rich texture and complex organic unity"[14] and a work in which "complexity . . . is rare."[15] How are these different and often contradictory interpretations to be reconciled? One 1989 essay, while it does not reconcile them, at least suggests a way to account for their differences; in "*The Marble Faun* and the Space of American Letters," Henry S. Sussman remarks that Hawthorne's novel is "a veritable program of contemporary theoretical interests and themes."[16]

This insight suggests one of the governing principles of the *multiple* readings of *The Marble Faun* that will be presented in the chapters to follow: that different theoretical interests and critical methods and vocabularies enable readers to construct strikingly different understandings of the novel. *The Marble Faun* has, in fact, shown this flexibility throughout its critical history, which is why I have entitled this chapter on its reception "Critical Transformations." Criticism and various sorts of transformation are crucial subjects of Hawthorne's novel. Because of its multiplicity, its mixing of genres, and its complex relationship to the changing systems of meaning and belief by which Americans of the mid-nineteeth century made sense of their experience, the novel has also been the object of frequent critical transformation. This word that I use to describe the operations of readers upon the novel is also, we recall, one of the titles of the novel itself. We may take this double reference of the word *transformation* as a reminder that the identity of any work of literature is neither something that lies complete and immutable "in" the work itself nor something that is arbitrarily given to it or imposed on it by readers who stand "outside." Rather, it is something formed and reformed in the specific intellectual and emotional transactions between readers and the words they read and in the communicated history of those transactions. To work different critical transformations upon *The Marble Faun* is to discover the range of meanings it can hold and the identities it can assume. But even more important, it is also to gain insight into the processes that produce the meanings we live by and the identities we call our own.

Readings

4

The Fall of Man

In his famous essay "Experience" (1844), Emerson observed: "It is very unhappy, but too late to be helped, the discovery we have made, that we exist. That discovery is called the Fall of Man. Ever afterward, we suspect our instruments. We have learned that we do not see directly, but mediately, and that we have no means of correcting these colored and distorting lenses which we are, or of computing the amount of their errors" (Emerson, 487). Most of the traditionally recognized issues and themes of *The Marble Faun* are raised in this passage. Here, as in Hawthorne's novel, the loss of Paradise that is described in the biblical story (on which the Christian doctrine of Original Sin was founded) is taken to be a figure for the human condition, or for the process of realizing one's human identity. To be fully human is to have a consciousness of one's existence, a capacity to reflect on one's life, that is unavailable to other species. From this consciousness derive many powers: the power to judge and choose, to define our desires and act in accordance with them, to revise our course, and to produce images or representations of the world and our experience in it. But these powers, through the exercise of which we have made the world our domain, also alienate us from the world and from ourselves. Once we are conscious of our instrumental role in the world—the role our judgments, choices, desires, and representations play in shaping the "reality" we encounter—we have tasted the fruit of our own knowledge and have lost our innocence. What we then know is that we can never live naturally in the world, because we live through the instrument of our consciousness, and that we can never know the world in its immediacy, because we only apprehend it through our "colored and distorting lenses." Thus, Emerson suggests the bearing of the religious doctrine of the Fall upon several potentially secular issues: the question of what it means to be human; the problem of interpretation; the function of art. In this chapter I will begin to untangle these thematic strands of *The Marble Faun*.

Readers of *The Marble Faun*, from its first appearance, have most frequently understood it to be an allegory of the Fall of Man. In this interpretation, the novel's central character is the young Italian rustic, Donatello, whose commission of an impulsive crime initiates him into the knowledge of good and evil and transforms him from a state of animal simplicity and innocence to one of human complexity and guilt. The plot also involves a secondary enactment of the Fall: the American copyist Hilda, a "daughter of the Puritans" (54) whose "angelic purity" (366) has set her apart from the other characters, accidentally witnesses Donatello's crime and thereby comes to share the human burden of the consciousness of sin. Stained by this knowledge, Hilda loses her aloof self-sufficiency and her capacity to reproduce the paintings of the Old Masters in their "pristine glory" (59) or even to perceive them as "miracles" (57). In exchange, she is invited to enter into the community of human sympathy and need that is established through the acknowledgment of our common imperfection.

A critical analysis of *The Marble Faun*, then, logically begins with the highly visible theme of the Fall. Which elements of the work contribute to the elaboration of this theme, and which appear unconnected or inconsistent with it? (This is a crucial question to ask about any literary interpretation and a way to begin to test its adequacy.) Here, the theme is primarily conveyed by the major events and general outline of the novel's plot. The opening scene introduces the reader to four friends congregated in the sculpture gallery of the Capitol in Rome. Two of these characters, the sculptor Kenyon and the painter Hilda, are young Americans who, like almost all aspiring American artists of the nineteenth century, have made their pilgrimage to learn from and work amidst the great treasures of European art. A third, Miriam, is also a painter, but unlike Hilda she produces undisciplined, original, and even idiosyncratic paintings—which often deal with violence, corruption, or alienation—rather than sublime copies of famous masterpieces. Neither is Miriam a daughter of the Puritans. Her origins are mysterious yet almost certainly non-American, and she exudes not angelic purity but worldly experience, sexuality, and sorrow. The fourth character is Donatello, a child of the Tuscan Hills and the last count of the venerable Italian family of Monte Benis. Donatello, the only member of the party who is not an artist, stands in the role of nature's nobleman.

The novel's first event is the simultaneous perception of the three artists that their friend Donatello bears an uncanny resemblance to one of the sculptures in the gallery: an antique marble statue of a faun, attributed to the Greek sculptor Praxiteles. The sculpted faun, clad only in a lion's skin and carrying a rough-hewn woodland flute, "conveys the idea of an amiable and sensual creature, easy, mirthful, apt for jollity, yet not incapable of being touched by pathos" (9). It is a dream creature in which "the characteristics of the brute creation meet and combine with those of humanity" and "all the pleasantness of sylvan life . . . seem[s] to be mingled and kneaded into one substance, along with the kindred qualities in the human soul" (9–10). Or perhaps it is "no dream, but rather a poet's reminiscence of a period when man's affinity with Nature was more strict, and his fellowship with every living thing more intimate and dear" (10–11). This last sentence of the first chapter alludes, of course, to the state of perfect harmony known to humankind in the Garden of Eden.

At the request of his friends, Donatello throws himself into the attitude of the faun. In appearance and in character, he seems to be its fleshly embodiment. "So full of animal life as he was, so joyous in his deportment, so handsome, so physically well-developed, he made no impression of incompleteness, of maimed or stinted nature. And yet, in social intercourse, these familiar friends of his habitually and instinctively allowed for him, as for a child or some other lawless thing, exacting no strict obedience to conventional rules" (14). So innocent is Donatello of social conventions that even his speech is described as "an unshaped sort of utterance" (12), and often he prefers to communicate in "the natural language of gesture" (77). So free is he of the typical habits and burdens of consciousness that memory of the past and anticipation of the future rarely intrude on his spontaneous life in the present. Donatello, then, is early associated with two distinct forms of perfection: the perfection of physical nature and the perfection of an artistic idea. A question that these associations raise is whether either form constitutes a workable or appropriate model for human identity.

Being human, Donatello is neither quite as carefree as a faun nor as self-contained as marble. The limits of his joyful spontaneity and of his self-containment are marked, in fact, by the affection that he has conceived for his characterological opposite, Miriam. At moments, Miriam shares Donatello's high spirits, but she is often seized with fits of bitterness and depression that seem, like her unsettling paintings, to have their source in some terrible episode of her secret past. In the novel's third chapter, "Subterranean Reminiscences," the memory of that past—which, until then, Miriam had generally been able to banish from her consciousness—returns in the form of a fifth character, who becomes known as Miriam's model. The scene is the Catacomb of Saint Calixtus, an underground cemetery that elaborately displays human mortality and suggestively symbolizes as well the human unconscious, filled with repressed images of corruption and death. Miriam becomes lost in the maze of vaults and finally reappears, followed by a strange man whom she appears to know and fear. Afterward, this man hovers around the edges of the community of artists in Rome, sometimes working as a model for Miriam or another painter, but always staying close to Miriam, who seems powerless either to acknowledge or to dismiss him. Donatello instinctively hates him.

The Fall of Man

The Fall occurs at midnight. A company of artists has taken a moonlight tour of Rome's historic sites, ending at the summit of the Tarpeian Rock, from which traitors were hurled to their deaths in ancient times. Miriam, who has been shadowed by her model throughout the evening, lingers on the precipice after the others have disbanded. Donatello waits with her. When the model again approaches, Donatello seizes him, looks for an instant at Miriam, who meets his gaze, and hurls her tormentor over the edge. In the immediate aftermath, this passionate deed—committed by Donatello's hands but approved by Miriam's eyes—"[brings] their two hearts together, till the horrour and agony of each was combined into one emotion, and that, a kind of rapture. . . . It was closer than a marriage-bond. So intimate, in those first moments, was the union, that it seemed as if their new sympathy annihilated all other ties, and that they were released from the chain of humanity" (174). They soon discover, however, that the opposite is the case, that "an individual wrongdoing melts into the great mass of human crime, and makes us—who dreamed only of our little separate sin—makes us guilty of the whole. And thus Miriam and her lover were not an insulated pair, but members of an innumerable confraternity of guilty ones, all shuddering at each other" (177). Donatello cannot bear the weight of the sins of the world that his sudden loss of innocence forces upon him; recoiling from his deed and from Miriam, he returns alone and in despair to his ancestral home.

On the night of the murder, Hilda has begun to descend with the others when she decides to go back for Miriam, who has been especially agitated all evening and may, Hilda thinks, welcome a sympathetic ear. Reaching the summit, she witnesses Miriam's and Donatello's exchange of glances and its consequence and departs unnoticed. The next day, Miriam seeks her in her rooms on the uppermost floor of an old tower, where she lives surrounded by doves and, though not a Catholic, tends the lamp of a rooftop shrine of the Virgin Mary. Hilda reveals what she has seen the night before and repels her former friend. "I am a poor, lonely girl, whom God has set here in an evil world, and given her only a white robe, and bid her wear it back to Him, as white as when she put it on," she tells Miriam. "Your powerful magnetism would be too much for me. The pure, white atmosphere, in which I try to discern what things are good and true, would be discoloured" (208).

At this point, the prelapsarian community of friends has broken down and they begin to wander. All but Hilda leave Rome, whose gardens—with the arrival of summer—have become breeding grounds for malaria. "Thus," the narrator remarks, "the scene is like Eden in its loveliness; like Eden, too, in the fatal spell that removes it beyond the scope of man's actual possessions" (73). Kenyon, the only one who knows nothing of the crime and throughout the novel "little more than surmise[s]" (382) what has so changed his friends, pays a long-planned visit to Donatello in the country. The young count has turned brooding and cynical. The animals in the woods around the Monte Beni estate, who had once responded to Donatello's call and sported with him as with any other wild companion, now flee him. Kenyon does not know how to assist his friend, until he encounters Miriam, who has come secretly to Monte Beni. Believing that she and Dona-tello must together face their remorse, their punishment, and whatever other consequences of their deed lie in store for them, Miriam asks Kenyon to help her arrange one last opportunity for Donatello to see her and accept, for better or worse, their union. He agrees to take Donatello on a ramble through the countryside and to lead him at the end of two weeks to the square in Perugia, where Miriam will meet them. Donatello's spirits are partly restored by the journey and by the acts of contrition that he performs at every roadside shrine. When Miriam presents herself in Perugia under the bronze statue of Pope Julius the Third, Donatello takes her hand, and Kenyon gives his bless-ing to a relationship meant "not, for earthly bliss . . . but for mutual elevation and encouragement towards a severe and painful life" (322).

Meanwhile, Hilda—while too pure still to be susceptible to ma-laria, Hawthorne's figure for humanity's heritage of sin—languishes in empty Roman picture galleries. The galleries are empty not only of companions for Hilda but also of inspiration. She no longer can take pleasure in her art, and the masterpieces that she once held to be sacred now seem to her profane. Although her conscience is not stained by guilt, her consciousness is. As the first rhyme in *The New England Primer*—the book from which generations of Hawthorne's Puritan ancestors learned to read—put it: "In Adam's fall / We sinned all." Or, as Hawthorne's narrator remarks of the murder's effect on Hilda: "Every crime destroys more Edens than our own!" (212). In Saint Peter's Hilda observes a woman emerging from confession looking peaceful and joyous. Suddenly overwhelmed by the burden of her own knowledge, she enters a confessional and pours out the story to an English-speaking priest. The priest realizes Hilda is not a Catholic, and when she resists his efforts to convert her he tells her that, because she was ineligible to receive the holy ordinance, there is no seal of the confessional and he is obliged to make her evidence known.

Returning to Rome on the day of Hilda's confession, Kenyon, who has loved her from the start, finds her less unapproachable than she had been before. He has even begun to receive signs of her receptiveness to his love, when she disappears. Unaware that she has been detained by the Roman authorities, Kenyon searches for her frantically. Miriam and Donatello, who have also returned to Rome, come to the Americans' rescue. Traveling in disguise, they reveal themselves to Kenyon and tell him that Hilda will be returned to him during the Roman carnival. They do not tell him that they have agreed to ransom her by giving themselves up. The trade occurs, and Miriam and Donatello submit themselves to Roman justice while Hilda and Kenyon prepare to exchange Rome and their artistic ambitions for the quiet but solid happiness of domestic life in America.

As this summary suggests, the events and language of *The Marble Faun* insistently recall the story of the Fall. The biblical theme is implicit in the figure of the unspoiled faun, who bears the potential for moral development. It is foreshadowed, well before the model's murder, in the sylvan dance that Donatello and Miriam perform in the Borghese Gardens. Their dance is said to offer "a glimpse . . . into the Golden Age, before mankind was burthened with sin and sorrow" (84), yet in a postlapsarian world it can only be an artificial escape from—or a superficial mask for—the fact of mortality. "It was like the sculptured scene on the front and sides of a sarcophagus, where, as often as any other device, a festive procession mocks the ashes and white bones that are treasured up, within" (88). After sin and sorrow descend upon Donatello, Miriam casts herself as Eve to his Adam when she asks Kenyon at Monte Beni to help her fulfill her lot of "complete self-sacrifice for his sake" so that "she, most wretched, who beguiled him into evil, might guide him to a higher innocence than that from which he fell" (283). And, finally, in case it was possible to miss the motif, Hawthorne has Miriam explicitly point it out to Kenyon as they observe the transformed Donatello: "The story of the Fall of Man! Is it not repeated in our Romance of Monte Beni?" (434).

The novel's ceaseless effort to dictate its own interpretation might itself be cause to question the confidence or the honesty of its claim that the theme of the Fall lies at its heart. But over the years more critics than not have accepted this claim, largely because it seemed consistent both with the Puritan heritage that was generally held to be so important a component of Hawthorne's imagination and with the evidence of his earlier fiction. Introducing the volume of Hawthorne's selected works that he edited in 1934, Austin Warren reiterated an earlier critic's remark about Hawthorne's "inveterate love of allegory" and explained this allegorical habit as "a subtler aspect of his Puritan didacticism" (Cohen, 177). "How could a descendant of the Puritans turn artist without utter betrayal of his heritage?" Warren asked. "Certainly not by celebrating the landscape or glorifying the human form. But, by the reduction of material objects to the status of tokens shadowing forth to the senses the spiritual states of men, he might effect a moralization of the natural world" (Cohen, 177–78). The first precept of the severe theology of John Calvin to which Hawthorne's Puritan ancestors subscribed was original depravity—the communication of sinfulness to every human being, from generation to generation, through Adam's violation of his covenant with God. This was the source of all the selfish and unlawful impulses to which human nature was prone, the cause of human mortality itself, and the basis of the need for redemption by God's grace and Christ's sacrifice. A Puritan-turned-artist, it was logical to expect, would produce fiction in which, as Hyatt Waggoner put it in 1963, "Eden [would never be] far in the background" (Cohen, 243).

Ideas and images associated with the Fall, moreover, had figured prominently in Hawthorne's earlier works. As Waggoner noted: "Loss of innocence, initiation into the complexities of experience in a world of ambiguously mingled good and evil, experiences of guilt so obscurely related to specific acts as to seem more 'original' and necessary than avoidable, these had been his subjects in story after story" (Cohen, 243). "My Kinsman, Major Molineux" (1832) depicts young America's disobedience to the authority of its British fatherland as a passage out of a protected, childlike state into both mature independence and guilty experience. "Young Goodman Brown" (1835) explores the strange compulsion of its title character to walk once with the devil in the forest, an appointment passed down from father to son and kept in each generation, and one that forever taints the union between Brown and his wife Faith. "The Birthmark" (1843) and "Rappaccini's Daughter" (1844) are concerned with godlike scientists who try to reverse the Fall but whose vain attempts to construct artificial Edens or to remove the mark of human mortality only confirm the limits they set out to exceed. And *The Blithedale Romance* (1852) satirizes the efforts of reformers, oblivious to their own inevitably impure motives and flawed perceptions, to re-create Paradise on earth through social engineering.

The most famous Fall in Hawthorne's previous works, however, is that of the godly minister Arthur Dimmesdale, whose moment of adulterous passion with Hester Prynne in *The Scarlet Letter* (1850) first acquaints him with sin as an inner reality rather than an abstraction. A significant consequence of Dimmesdale's sin and guilt is that they seem to make him a better minister, more inspiring in his expressions of the need for salvation and more responsive and sympathetic to the troubles and failings of others. This development of his character raises a question in *The Scarlet Letter* that becomes the central issue in *The Marble Faun*'s treatment of the loss of innocence: the question of the Fortunate Fall. Are we to understand the loss of humankind's original simplicity, innocence, and immortality not so much as a punishment that everyone repeatedly and fatally receives but as the opportunity to experience the moral choice, personal growth, and sympathy for others that make us fully human? Was the Fall, ultimately, fortunate?

This question is debated by the characters of *The Marble Faun* and by its critics. After stating that "our Romance of Monte Beni" repeats the story of the Fall, Miriam articulates the Fortunate Fall—or *felix culpa*—position: "And may we follow the analogy yet farther? Was that very sin—into which Adam precipitated himself and all his race—was it the destined means by which, over a long pathway of toil and sorrow, we are to attain a higher, brighter, and profounder happiness, than our lost birthright gave? Will not this idea account for the permitted existence of sin, as no other theory can?" (434–35). By the time Miriam openly proposes the idea, however, Hawthorne has thoroughly familiarized his reader with its gist. Donatello is early described as "a creature in a state of development less than what mankind has attained" (78), a being of "clear simplicity" whose "imperfectly developed intellect" lacks "the dark element" (79–80) necessary to its fulfillment. Later, in guilty seclusion at Monte Beni, Donatello seems to have lost his resemblance to the faun, but when Kenyon suggests that, whatever his personal pain, he might still find meaning in living for others, "the original beauty, which sorrow had partly effaced, came back elevated and spiritualized. In the black depths, the Faun had a soul, and was struggling with it towards the light of Heaven" (268). It is this struggle that Kenyon unconsciously captures in his clay bust of Donatello when he changes the "distorted and violent look" (272) that the sculpted features momentarily assume into an expression reminiscent "of the antique faun, but now illuminated with a higher meaning, such as the old marble never bore" (274).

Hilda's transformation may also be seen to support the idea of *felix culpa* and to suggest Hawthorne's greater concern with the social consequences of original sin for humankind than with its theological significance. In the severity of her moral and aesthetic judgments, Hilda appears to the other characters to resemble one of the cherubim with flaming swords sent by God to enforce Adam and Eve's expulsion from the Garden. Miriam's early remark that "[her] innocence is like a sharp steel sword" (66) is echoed when Kenyon tells Hilda that she separates right from wrong "with the remorselessness of a steel blade" (384). Miriam fills out this image in her response to being expelled from Hilda's life after the night at the Tarpeian Rock: "You have no sin, nor any conception of what it is; and therefore you are so terribly severe! As an angel, you are not amiss; but, as a human creature, and a woman among earthly men and women, you need a sin to soften you!" (209). To some degree, Miriam and Donatello's deed itself provides the conception of sin that softens Hilda, bringing her sufficiently into the community of "earthly men and women" to receive and return Kenyon's affection. This need and capacity for sympathy, some critics have argued, is the consequence of—and compensation for—the Fall that most interested Hawthorne and that he meant his readers to enact in their readings of his works. As Gordon Hutner has put it, in a world without divine revelation, human communion must fill the void. Hawthorne's habitual secrets, mysteries, and moral ambiguities cannot be analytically penetrated or judgmentally disposed of by his characters or his readers. They can, however, prompt a commitment to "an ideal of sympathy as an imperative for both aesthetic and social experience," a commitment that will not dissolve our bondage to sin and sorrow but will strengthen and comfort us in our bonds to one another.[1]

The Marble Faun thus repeatedly advances the doctrine of the Fortunate Fall and offers its reader several bases on which to interpret it in light of that doctrine. But this interpretation encounters some serious difficulties. First, it is expressly rejected at the end of the novel by Hawthorne's American characters and, implicitly, by his narrator. When Kenyon tentatively repeats to Hilda the moral that Miriam has drawn from Donatello's development, her response is swift and decisive: "This is terrible; and I could weep for you, if you indeed believe it. Do you not perceive what a mockery your creed makes, not only of all religious sentiment, but of moral law, and how it annuls and obliterates whatever precepts of Heaven are written deepest within us?

You have shocked me beyond words!" (460). Kenyon hastily recants: "Forgive me, Hilda! . . . I never did believe it! But the mind wanders wild and wide; and so lonely as I live and work, I have neither pole-star above, nor light of cottage-windows here below, to bring me home. . . . Oh, Hilda, guide me home!" (460–61). The narrator identifies himself as a friend of Hilda's and Kenyon's, and in the postscript that Hawthorne added for the novel's second printing, he includes himself in the scene: "We three had climbed to the top of Saint Peter's, and were looking down upon the Rome which we were soon to leave, but which (having already sinned sufficiently in that way) it is not my purpose further to describe" (464). The Americans have regained their moral altitude, and the narrator, like Kenyon, is ready to renounce sin and art and follow Hilda home.

A second problem for the doctrine of *felix culpa* is that the novel never directly represents, and does not seem particularly interested in, Donatello's intellectual and moral growth. We see a depressed Donatello at Monte Beni but never come to know the mature, intellectually sophisticated, or morally complex Donatello that his loss of innocence supposedly produces. The only material evidence of his growth is Kenyon's clay bust—an unfinished work of art that, as we have seen, assumed the expression of a humanized faun entirely by accident. In a sense, Donatello remains what he started out as: not a mature human agent but an embodied idea, a representation produced by the "suspect . . . instruments" of others' imaginations, susceptible to re-production or transformation in accordance with their changing perceptions.

To view Donatello as an embodied idea, a work of art, or a model for artistic transformation is also to recognize his affinity with the character he kills. Upon his first appearance, Miriam's model is described as "[looking] as if he might just have stept out of a picture, and, in truth, [he] was likely enough to find his way into a dozen pictures; being no other than one of those living models, dark, bushy bearded, wild of aspect and attire, whom artists convert into Saints or assassins, according as their pictorial purposes demand" (19). This wild model is also said to resemble the "antique Satyrs" (30), those "rough cousins" (78) to the fauns, one of whom was the legendary progenitor of the Monte Beni line (233). Donatello's association with the model clouds Miriam's image of his development toward "a higher, brighter, and profounder happiness" and knowledge; it suggests that his course in the novel should be plotted not as a linear progression but as a cyclical repetition. In fact, when Donatello kills the model, he replicates in his own new relation to Miriam the relationship between Miriam and the model from which he sought to free her. Donatello thus assumes the role of the model, whose mysterious bond to Miriam is repeatedly suggested to involve a bloody deed of which he was the author and she was—or appeared to be—indirectly guilty. This suggestion of the model's crime, which in turn models Donatello's, is reinforced by Miriam's pointed resemblance to the historical figure Beatrice Cenci. Beatrice, whose significance to *The Marble Faun* will be discussed in greater depth in chapter 6, was the daughter of a sixteenth-century Italian nobleman; she was executed for conspiring with her older brother Giacomo to kill the father who had brutalized them both and possibly had raped her.

One way of accounting for the contradictions and inconsistencies in Hawthorne's treatment of the theme of the Fall is to argue, as Richard Harter Fogle did, that Hawthorne "neither accepts nor rejects" the idea of *felix culpa* but "leaves the question in suspension. . . . The suspension between opposite beliefs is the life-principle of *The Marble Faun*."[2] This dialectical solution is consistent with the general sense of Hawthorne's dividedness or bipolarity that, as we noted at the outset, almost every reader of his works has in one way or another shared. But it presumes that the theological *question* was important enough to Hawthorne to constitute a "life-principle" of his novel and that he held strong "opposite beliefs" about the meaning of original sin. This presumption is borne out neither by Hawthorne's life—he did not attend church and showed little sign of religious devotion—nor, I think, by his art. Hawthorne himself suggests a more appropriate understanding of the function of the Fall in his novel when he identifies his title character, the fortunately or unfortunately falling Donatello, with the unnamed model "whom artists convert into Saints or assassins, according as their pictorial purposes demand." The Fall itself is a kind of model, one that helps Hawthorne give form to other pressing literary purposes. Indeed, the earlier works to which the model of the Fall contributes address a variety of more concrete and topical concerns: family conflict; the psychological causes of revolution; the use of spectral evidence in the Salem witch trials; the American ideals of self-creation and social perfectibility; and, pervasively, problems of sexual identity and relations. The Fall, that is, serves Hawthorne as a useful organizational device, a way of grounding the plots and themes of his fiction in one of the most familiar plots and resonant themes his culture possessed.

As an issue in itself, the Fall was not at the heart of Hawthorne's intellectual or imaginative life. By the time he wrote *The Marble Faun*, moreover, theological controversies concerning the Fall had lost most of their popular force and interest. As Richard Brodhead has pointed out, the reading of the Fall that Donatello's supposed development suggests, and that Miriam articulates, "[was] certainly not novel: already well established long before Milton, it was a humanistic truism in the nineteenth century. But the curiosity of *The Marble Faun* is that Hilda finds the doctrine of the *felix culpa* new and inexpressibly shocking."[3] Why does Hawthorne seem to construct a drama whose purpose is to affirm an old truism? Why are his characters awed or shocked by "so platitudinous a message" (Brodhead, 77)? And then, why does the narrator, along with Hilda, appear to undo the novel's design and deny that the truism is true after all? No reading of the Fall will answer these questions for us. To answer them convincingly, we will have to discover what is ignored, suppressed, or abstracted by the allegory of the Fall in *The Marble Faun* and by critical interpretations that center on that theme.

Playing out the significance of what is ignored, suppressed, or abstracted by the novel's dominant motif and by much of its criticism will be the project of the next three chapters. In the closing pages of this one, though, we may demonstrate the need for that project, and begin to define its direction, by pointing to some of the elements of *The Marble Faun* that challenge the adequacy or the validity of its characterization as "the story of the Fall of Man." Adam's sin is disobedience to the perfect Father who has created him in His image and Who has offered him, in exchange for filial reverence, a life in Paradise. But in *The Marble Faun,* the association of Donatello with Miriam's model, and of both with the Cenci case, suggests a world in which—before Donatello, or even the model, has sinned—fathers are evil. This suggestion is constantly reinforced in the novel's treatment of its class of spiritual "Fathers" and ostensible representatives of God, the Roman Catholic priests. Hawthorne describes Rome as the home of "the Papal despotism" (109) and as a city in thrall to "an irresponsible dynasty of Holy Fathers" (100). When Hilda vanishes, Kenyon goes so far as to fear that she may have been raped by one or more of "a priesthood, pampered, sensual, with red and bloated cheeks, and carnal eyes" (411). Clearly, the Father's covenant with the son that establishes the necessary condition for the Fall is complicated by the historical setting and social attitudes represented in Hawthorne's story.

When we read *The Marble Faun* through the "colored and distorting lens" of the Fall, we are also likely not to perceive that it is a story more centrally about daughters and fathers than it is about fathers and sons. In the novel's opening paragraph, before Donatello or the statue of the faun appears, Hawthorne introduces the question of humankind's moral destiny by way of a different sculpture: "Here, likewise, is seen a symbol (as apt, at this moment, as it was two thousand years ago) of the Human Soul, with its choice of Innocence or Evil close at hand, in the pretty figure of a child, clasping a dove to her bosom, but assaulted by a snake" (5). The first representative of the human soul, then, is a female child; it is interesting, too, that the "choice" with which she seems to be presented is not between remaining innocent and doing evil but between denying and resisting the evil that already assaults her. This image evokes the figure of Beatrice Cenci and the choices of Miriam and Hilda more than it does the faun and Donatello's deed. And, in fact, the painted image of Beatrice Cenci is a more prominent and recurrent symbol in the novel than is the marble faun. Over and over, Beatrice's image insinuates a dark mystery that primarily involves—and may proceed from the relationship between—fathers and daughters. This relationship wildly proliferates in *The Marble Faun,* moving outward from the Cenci legend to encompass Miriam's bondage to her model and deference to the bronze pontiff in Perugia and Hilda's reproductive service to the Old Masters and confession to the English-speaking priest.

The multiplication of morally ambiguous fathers and father figures in *The Marble Faun* signifies another problem for the critical tradition that follows from James Russell Lowell's description of the novel as a "parable of the development of the Christian idea." After encountering the priests, the venerated religious painters, the sculpted popes, Kenyon's bust of John Milton, and Hilda's Puritan God, we are prompted to ask: which Christian idea? Christianity itself is divided here into the contrasting ideologies and aesthetics of Catholicism and Protestantism. As we will see in the next chapter, the threat of European Catholicism was a popular concern of the guardians of American Protestant culture in the mid-nineteenth century. The biblical theme of the Fall provides no insight into the ways in which this cultural context bears on Hawthorne's novel. Nor does it register another dimension, or complication, of "the Christian idea" in *The Marble Faun*—the idea of the Jew. Hawthorne's American Protestants are not only immersed in a Catholic culture but spend much of the latter half of the novel traversing Rome's Jewish ghetto. And Miriam, whose secret past precipitates all the action and whose raven hair emanates "a dark glory such as crowns no Christian maiden's head" (48), is conceived as a Jew and modeled on a Jewish woman whom Hawthorne met in Europe and by whom he was deeply unsettled.

Finally, we may note that Rome is identified both as "the Eternal City" (213), the home of Christianity, and as the "home of art" (214), and that a great deal of the novel's attention is focused on the production, reception, and effects of works of art. The relative powers and values of sculpture, painting, and literature are examined, and it is often the issue of artistic originality rather than the issue of original sin that seems to lie at the heart of the book. This aspect of *The Marble Faun* not only provides an alternative focal point to that of the Fall but may be seen to critique the historical and theological claims that are implicit in the idea of the Fall. That idea posits a moment of innocence and naturalness, the loss of which marks the beginning of human civilization. It implies, therefore, that a common origin and a shared essence underlie the apparent differences and distortions of human experience and character. But even as it draws heavily on the idea and implications of the Fall, Hawthorne's novel depicts a world that is not so much divided between nature and civilization as it is constructed by an array of overlapping artistic representations, each as artificial as the next. It is a world in which efforts to uncover original sources only multiply the models and images that stand in for them, and perhaps are all there is to them. What appear to be passages— back to the genesis of the Monte Beni line, to the truth of Miriam's past, to the divine springs of the works by Hilda's Old Masters—turn out to be halls of mirrors. And the "true" vision or knowledge with which Hilda is sometimes credited inevitably is won not by perfect openness to human experience but by selective repression of it.

In his final weeks of composing *The Marble Faun*, Hawthorne sent his publisher a list of possible titles and asked him "to select one of them, or imagine something better." The nominees included "The Romance of a Faun," "Monte Beni: A Romance," "Miriam: A Romance," "Hilda: A Romance," "Donatello: A Romance," and "Marble and Life / Man; A Romance" (196). Hawthorne added that, if possible, he did not wish "to make the fantastic aspect of the book too prominent by putting the Faun into the title page" (*CE*, 18:197). We can only speculate on the difference it would have made to the novel's critical history had one of these titles—say "Miriam: A Romance" or "Marble and Life"—been chosen. In any event, the range of options that Hawthorne offered to James T. Fields suggests the multiple interests, attitudes, and purposes that compete for dominance in *The Marble Faun*. In *The Scarlet Letter*, Hester Prynne broods over the lawlessness and mutability of her daughter Pearl and feels "like one who has evoked a spirit, but, by some irregularity in the process of conjuration, has failed to win the master-word that should control this new and incomprehensible intelligence" (*CE*, 1:93). Hawthorne, likewise, never won the "master-word" with which to domesticate his artistic production, *The Marble Faun,* and this is why even an inter-pretation explicitly endorsed by the work itself is a critical *transfor-mation* of it.

Reading the novel as an allegory of the Fall transforms it by ig-noring or deemphasizing its setting, its aesthetic self-consciousness, its women, its disturbing autobiographical sources and resonances, and its participation in the construction of America's religious, ethnic, and cultural self-image. George Edward Woodberry exemplified and ra-tionalized this transformation when he wrote in 1918 that Donatello's crime "is not a particular crime, with a history and explanation of its own, but a sin,—sin in the abstract. Any other crime would have served the purpose."[4] Hyatt Waggoner, among many others, reenacted it when he wrote in 1963: "There is too *much* of Rome, and too much about art. They are a burden the story is simply incapable of carrying" (Cohen, 255). These judgments are apt *if,* and only if, we assume that the important story here, the real story, is the Fall. If this is the case, then the historical and aesthetic matters and the specifically sexual component of the novel's crimes, fears, and fantasies are obstructions, burdens, distractions from the "abstract" meaning of *The Marble Faun.* My assumption, though, is different: For various reasons and in various forms (some of which I outlined in chapter 1), Hawthorne was confronted during his years in Europe with a "new and incomprehen-sible intelligence" that shaped his last completed romance in ways he did not fully control or recognize. The allegory of the Fall is not the essence of this new intelligence but an old organizational principle—drawn from his previous works and from the cultural order that his European experience challenged—that Hawthorne hopes will grant him the "master-word" over *The Marble Faun.* Had it effectively done so, the novel would have offered us far less to write and think about.

5

Catholic Propensities

In the opening pages of *The Marble Faun*, Hawthorne defines "that state of feeling which is experienced oftenest at Rome" in the following way: "It is a vague sense of ponderous remembrances; a perception of such weight and density in a by-gone life, of which this spot was the centre, that the present moment is pressed down or crowded out, and our individual affairs and interests are but half as real, here, as elsewhere" (6). The interpretation of the novel based on the Fall of Man may be seen as the critical equivalent of this experience of Rome. It gives precedence to a weighty, central myth—the story of the Fall— to which it subordinates the elements of the novel that express "the present moment" in which Hawthorne wrote and the "individual affairs and interests" of his characters. In this chapter we will turn our attention from archetypal sources and mythic structures in *The Marble Faun* to Hawthorne's present moment in Rome, its social and biographical contexts, and its representation in his characters' struggles to reconcile or choose between competing forms of Christianity and of art.

Writing in the magazine *Catholic World* in 1885, Father A. F. Hewitt remarked that in Rome, for the first time, Hawthorne had been "brought face to face with Catholicism" and had had "his mind freed to a considerable extent from Protestant prejudices."[1] Other critics have disagreed, most notably Roger Asselineau, who granted Hawthorne's fascination with Catholic history, ritual, and art during his Italian residence but acidly contended in his essay "Hawthorne Abroad" that "his arteries were too much hardened by the time he decided to travel" and that, with a few exceptions, his encounter with Catholicism produced "the standard reactions of an American Protestant of his time" (Pearce 1964, 371, 378). What seems indisputable is that Hawthorne's encounter with Catholicism was an ambivalent one, that it was a significant element of his Italian experience, and that both its significance and Hawthorne's ambivalence are apparent in *The Marble Faun*. There is ample evidence for these claims. Descriptions of and commentaries on Catholic sites, practices, and clergy fill the notebooks that Hawthorne kept in Italy and often appear, with minimal revisions, in the novel. When Kenyon is said to be "deeply disturbed by his idea of [Hilda's] Catholic propensities" (368), Hawthorne is drawing on his own disturbance over his daughter Una's sudden interest in religious forms and ceremonies and over what he described in his notebooks as the "alarming fervor of her love for Rome" (*CE*, 14:230). Yet in the novel the perceived threat of Catholicism to these young "daughter[s] of the Puritans" is countered to some degree by the comfort Hilda takes in confession—at a moment when, as she tells Kenyon, "I must either have done what you saw me doing, or have gone mad" (368)—and by the fact that Hilda returns from her period of captivity unconverted and unharmed.

As Robert S. Levine has pointed out recently, anti-Catholic sentiment, rhetoric, and literature were prominent features of American cultural life in the early nineteenth century. American Protestants tended to share the opinion expressed by John Adams in an 1821 letter to Thomas Jefferson "that a free government and the Roman Catholick [*sic*] religion can never exist together in any nation or country," and many believed, or were ever ready to believe, in the existence of "a Roman Catholic conspiracy to gain the republic as the crown jewel of the papal kingdom."[2] Increasing rates of Catholic immigration in every decade prior to the Civil War intensified these fears and helped produce a large market for virulent nativist tracts and for gothic fiction featuring Catholic villains. The most notable form of such fiction was the convent novel. Purportedly true accounts of the captivity of young innocents in North American outposts of Catholic conspiracy and degeneracy, works such as Rebecca Theresa Reed's *Six Months in a Convent* (1835) and Maria Monk's *Awful Disclosures of the Hotel Dieu Nunnery* (1836) "revealed" the world hidden behind convent walls: a world of torture, slavery, and sexual perversion, of novitiates raped by priests in confessional, of babies smothered, and of plots to take control of the United States through mass conversion of its unsuspecting citizens (Levine, 110–12).

Levine argues that the discourse of anti-Catholicism had a cultural currency and force in Hawthorne's time that made it "tempting [and] available to any author of the period, particularly a writer of historical romance, like Hawthorne, who explicitly addressed the role of Protestant-Catholic conflict in early American history" (Levine, 106). There is no evidence that Hawthorne gave credence to the idea of a Roman Catholic conspiracy in America, but in early historical tales such as "The Gray Champion" (1835) and "Endicott and the Red Cross" (1838), he does link "the Puritan suspicion of Catholicism to the impulses guiding the colonists toward the Revolution" (Levine, 120). Thus, Hawthorne draws, however moderately, on the popular discourse of anti-Catholicism as a way of dramatizing the origins of American nationality and as a way of establishing his community with the reading public.

Xenophobia is a powerful tool for creating a sense of national community in troubled and divided times. And nativist writers of the antebellum period used the fear of foreign Catholics to bolster Protestant America's insecure sense of itself as a unified community. Ironically, though, the Catholic Church that these writers portrayed as a deadly threat to American community was itself a kind of model of the purposeful, coherent, and secure community that Americans increasingly felt they lacked. Convents were places that accommodated spiritual, economic, and domestic life and fulfilled the needs belonging to each of these spheres—spheres that seemed less and less integrated or even compatible to many citizens of Jacksonian America. Those who demonized the Church and its convents, then, were often struggling with their forbidden and perhaps unconscious attraction not necessarily to the Catholic religion but to the ideal of communal order and stability with which they associated it. The convent novel controls this attraction to the communal ideal of convent life by representing Catholic community as a diabolical instrument for the violation and ultimate destruction of Protestant and American individuality.

Then, as now, individual freedom was a sacred concept (if not always a reality) of American political life. But the felt loss of community and connectedness that I discussed briefly in chapter 1 was a powerful counterforce to America's dominant valuation of individual autonomy over social relationship. The need for more meaningful and satisfying forms of social connectedness gave rise in the 1840s to a rash of religious and political communitarian movements. Hawthorne himself invested and for a time resided in the utopian socialist community at Brook Farm. The principal participants in the Brook Farm experiment were Transcendentalists and Unitarians, but they could not escape some awareness of what Levine calls "the homology between monastery and reform community" (Levine, 115). That homology, or structural correspondence, was made explicit in an 1846 article, "The Catholics and Associationists," written by the respected Unitarian minister and Brook Farm supporter William Henry Channing. Channing characterized the ideal life of a Brook Farmer as one "spent without one thought of self, in close and constant relations with his brethren," and he urged advocates of associationism to "regard with respect and sympathy the Catholic church, as the most successful attempt in the history of the world to bring the race into unity, however mistaken they may deem its measures" (Levine, 116–17).

By the time Hawthorne wrote *The Blithedale Romance* (1852), his novel based on the Brook Farm experiment, the community had long failed and a number of its members had converted to Catholicism. In that novel Hawthorne's narrator and ironic substitute, Miles Coverdale, presents a critique of Blithedale (Brook Farm) that is a subtler and somewhat less sensational version of the popular novelistic demonizations of convent life: the utopian Blithedale community consumes the individuality of its initiates, who are used and sometimes destroyed in the service not of spiritual ideals but of the corrupt and worldly ambitions of the community's leaders. Coverdale, the minor poet and detached individualist, is himself shown to be as manipulative and self-serving as the zealots he resists, and while he escapes with his identity intact, it is only to return to the isolation of his bachelor apartment and the triviality of his private life. Lonely and embittered, he remembers Blithedale as a corrupted dream, a mock paradise, but his time there remains the only moment of his life in which his need for community was satisfied; in a sense, Blithedale is the only home he has ever had.

In *The Marble Faun* the desire for and the fear of intimate community, and the question of what constitutes a home, are again played out—this time much more directly—through the relationships of Hawthorne's characters to the ideas and the institutions of Catholicism. The home of the Catholic Church, of course, is Rome, but neither Hawthorne nor any of his characters is at home there. The early letters and notebook entries that Hawthorne wrote in Rome convey his acute sense of being in an alien environment; one entry, in fact, summarizes his impression of the city in the word *un-home-likeness* (CE, 14:56). Yet at the same time, as I have indicated, Hawthorne was feeling emotionally as well as physically alienated from the United States and less at home with his own American sensibilities. Two months after his pronouncement of Rome's "un-home-likeness," he wrote to his friend William Ticknor that the city "has a sort of fascination which will make me reluctant to take a final leave of it," and then immediately added lines that suggest his understanding of this growing affinity for Rome as a kind of treason, a desire for expatriation: "I wish I were a little more patriotic; but to confess the truth, I had rather be a sojourner in any other country than return to my own. The United States are fit for many excellent purposes, but they certainly are not fit to live in" (CE, 18:140).

Hawthorne's novel can be seen to be built on this tension, this split, in the definition of home. "Home" in *The Marble Faun* is a contested territory to which America and Rome, Protestantism and Catholicism, middle-class marriage and the vocation of art, lay competing claims. The word itself appears again and again, most prominently in passages that represent the claims that Rome and Catholicism make on the allegiances of Hawthorne's American Protestants. Rome is called "this central home of the world" (213) and "this home of art" (214), and its universality is reinforced in its depictions as "the City of all time, and of all the world" (111) and "the Eternal City" (213). Similarly, the central monument of Catholicism, Saint Peter's, is described as religion's "material home" (351) and, in the title of a chapter devoted to it, as "The World's Cathedral." (Throughout his novel, Hawthorne inaccurately refers to this historic church as a cathedral; the bishop's seat, or cathedral church of the pope as bishop of Rome, is in fact Saint John Lateran.)

The more closely we look at these phrases, the more suspicious we may become that they are subtle equivocations rather than endorsements. The same sentence that deems Rome "the Eternal City" and the "central home of the world" contrasts it with the "native homes in England or America" (213) of the tourists who make up a large part of Rome's seasonal population. This comparison would suggest that Rome is the deeper and more spiritual home, yet its characterization as "the City of all time, and of all the world," may be read to imply the opposite: that Rome's claim is the claim of temporality, materiality, and worldliness rather than that of a "native" (in the sense of "original" or "essential") home. Hawthorne's representations of Saint Peter's also lend themselves to this skeptical reading. Does its description as the "material home" of religion imply that it is not a home for the true religious spirit? Is it "the world's cathedral" rather than God's? Organized around such questions as these, the conflict over the meaning of home in *The Marble Faun* is perhaps most directly posed in the pair of requests made of Hilda in the closing chapters. Attempting to make her a Catholic, the priest to whom she has confessed urges: "Come home, dear child—poor wanderer, who hast caught a glimpse of the heavenly light—come home, and be at rest!"

(362). Attempting to make her his wife, Kenyon pleads: "The mind wanders wild and wide; and so lonely as I live and work, I have neither pole-star above, nor light of cottage-windows here below, to bring me home. Were you my guide, my counsellor, my inmost friend, with that white wisdom which clothes you as with a celestial garment, all would go well. Oh, Hilda, guide me home!" (461).

The discovery that one is uncertain as to what is "homelike" and what is "unhomelike," or that the alien has become familiar and the familiar alien, is the experience that Freud defines as "the uncanny." The German word for uncanny is *unheimlich*—literally, "unhome-like"—and as Freud pointed out, the word's reference to that which is secret or private strangely (uncannily) duplicates one of the meanings of its opposite, *heimlich*.[3] The events and the atmosphere of *The Marble Faun* often exhibit qualities of the uncanny, as Freud defined it, and I will have more to say on this subject in chapter 7 when I discuss the role of repression in the novel. Here, the consciousnesses of characters whose sense of home is divided or doubled may be described by a related term, forms of which appear more than 50 times in the novel itself. That term is "haunted."

The word *haunt* and the word *home* are etymological cousins. Their connotations differ, however, in that a home implies a thoroughly domesticated place, one that is owned or securely possessed, whereas a haunt is a place to which one habitually returns but which is not domesticated or under one's private control. As an adjective, *haunted* describes a mind or a place that is possessed by what it possesses, one that has lost control of or that is controlled by what is inside of it. The related yet opposing connotations of these terms can help us to see how the struggle over the meaning of home in *The Marble Faun* involves questions of personal agency and freedom. A "home," as opposed to a "haunt," is associated with self-control and with security, but Hawthorne suggests that such a home may also be a static and conventional place that constrains expression and limits possibility. Kenyon observes of the prerogatives of American artists in Rome, for instance, that "the Papal despotism allows us freer breath than our native air" (109), and later, when Donatello's gloom begins to lift during his ramble in the countryside, the narrator terms him "homeless, and therefore free" (314). On the other hand, to be haunted is to lose a measure of control over oneself and one's environment, but it may also grant one access to wider and richer experience. Miriam, whose experience is wider, if not happier, and whose art is wilder than that of any of the other characters, produces "glimpses, sketches, and half-developed hints of beings and objects, grander and more beautiful than we can find anywhere in reality" in a studio that resembles nothing so much as "the outward type of a poet's haunted imagination" (41).

Catholic Rome appears in *The Marble Faun* as the haunted home of Christianity. It is a city built around ruins and over corpses and haunted by the ghosts of its past, by ancient grandeur and ancient crimes. It is also a city that haunts its visitors. It cannot be fully known or possessed, yet it takes possession of those who enter it and makes its "bygone life," its alien history, more familiar and immediate to them than their own existences, which seem "but half as real, here, as elsewhere." As Hilda remarks: "I sometimes fancy . . . that Rome— mere Rome—will crowd everything else out of my heart" (111). Hawthorne, like Hilda, finds Rome's and Catholicism's imperialistic claim on the emotions and imagination of the individual at once appealing and unacceptable. Nowhere is the nature of that claim and the basis for resisting it more subtly illustrated than in the long, brilliant passage describing Hilda's encounter with the symbol of imperial Roman Catholicism, Saint Peter's.

> Hilda had not always been adequately impressed by the grandeur of this mighty Cathedral. When she first lifted the heavy-leathern curtain, at one of the doors, a shadowy edifice in her imagination had been dazzled out of sight by the reality. Her pre-conception of Saint Peter's was a structure of no definite outline, misty in its architecture, dim and gray, and huge, stretching into an interminable perspective, and over-arched by a Dome like a cloudy firmament. Beneath that vast breadth and height, as she had fancied them, the personal man might feel his littleness, and the soul triumph in its immensity. So, in her earlier visits, when the compassed splendour

of the actual interiour glowed before her eyes, she had profanely called it a great prettiness; a gay piece of cabinet-work on a Titanic scale; a jewel-casket, marvelously magnified.

This latter image best pleased her fancy; a casket, all inlaid, in the inside, with precious stones of various hue, so that there should not be a hair's breadth of the small interiour unadorned with its resplendent gems. Then, conceive this minute wonder of a mosaic-box, increased to the magnitude of a Cathedral, without losing the intense lustre of its littleness, but all its petty glory striving to be sublime. The magic transformation from the minute to the vast has not been so cunningly effected, but that the rich adornment still counteracts the impression of space and loftiness. The spectator is more sensible of its limits than of its extent.

Until after many visits, Hilda continued to mourn for that dim, illimitable interiour, which, with her eyes shut, she had seen from childhood, but which had vanished at her first glimpse through the actual door. Her childish vision seemed preferable to the Cathedral which Michael Angelo, and all the great architects, had built; because, of the dream-edifice, she had said, 'How vast it is!'—while, of the real Saint Peter's, she could only say, 'After all, it is not so immense!' Besides, such as the church is, it can nowhere be made visible at one glance. It stands in its own way. You see an aisle or a transept; you see the nave, or the tribune; but, on account of its ponderous piers and other obstructions, it is only by this fragmentary process that you get an idea of the Cathedral.

There is no answering such objections. The great church smiles calmly upon its critics, and, for all response, says, 'Look at me!'— and if you still murmur for the loss of your shadowy perspective, there comes no reply, save, 'Look at me!'—in endless repetition, as the one thing to be said. And, after looking many times, with long intervals between, you discover that the Cathedral has gradually extended itself over the whole compass of your idea; it covers all the site of your visionary temple, and has room for its cloudy pinnacles beneath the Dome. (348–50)

Hilda's initial disappointment with Saint Peter's is a function of its very materiality. Throughout the passage, it is materiality and immediacy with which the church is repeatedly associated. In Hilda's childhood idea, Saint Peter's had resisted the limitations of material design: "dim" and "gray" and "misty," this "structure of no definite outline . . . over-arched by a Dome like the cloudy firmament" had served as her figure of spirituality, divinity, heaven itself. This vision expresses Hilda's strict Protestant differentiation of flesh from spirit and deemphasis of the life of the body in matters of the soul. Her preconceived Saint Peter's is, thus, a place where "the personal man might feel his littleness, and the soul triumph in its immensity." Yet, Hilda's emotional investment in this "fancied" church and her desire for a material embodiment of her religious idea in the first place suggest opposing "Catholic propensities."

The belittling image of Saint Peter's as an oversized jewel casket conveys Hilda's bitter sense of betrayal. She has found the basilica to be not an architectural expression of the immortal soul but a crammed box of earthly splendors, of "petty glory striving to be sublime." In addition to its connotation of worldliness, the image of the jewel casket, of course, is associated with mortality and with the excessively lavish encasement of the corrupt body rather than with the measureless "space and loftiness" necessary to house the soul. But there is also a vividness and a vitality here that had never really attached to the "shadowy edifice in her imagination [that] had been dazzled out of sight by the reality." If the real in one sense falls short of Hilda's imagining, in another it exposes Hilda's "childish vision" as an empty abstraction, a more or less image-less idea. In the dazzling light of the Catholic Church, this Protestant vision seems inescapably "dim" and fragile, which is why it "vanished at her first glimpse through the actual door."

The problem with the "interminable perspective" that Hilda's Saint Peter's is conceived to provide is that it is not aesthetically or psychologically possible, that is, it cannot be realized either in a work of art or by a human being. God's perspective is without boundaries, but in human terms the word *perspective* itself implies a particular and limited angle of vision; no perspective is available without limits because, in life and art, limits are what constitute perspectives. The actual Saint Peter's mediates between the ideal of the interminable, or what the passage elsewhere calls the "illimitable," and the reality of limited perspective. It does so by substituting a "fragmentary process" for Hilda's static, unitary, abstract, and unrealizable ideal. The church neither offers nor allows an "interminable perspective"; on the contrary, "it stands in its own way" so as to ensure that "it can nowhere be made visible at one glance." Thus, it is a religious structure adapted to the experience and the capacities of "the personal man [or woman]." Its overall idea is communicated only through multiple partial views, through repetition, and through the senses. Significantly, in the last paragraph of the passage, Saint Peter's is imagined to respond to its critics by insisting "in endless repetition" on its immediacy, its tangibility. And eventually, its sensory appeal—'Look at me!'—seems persuasive. Once dwarfed by Hilda's expansive idea, the cathedral now extends "over [its] whole compass," as the deft reversal in Hawthorne's closing sentence indicates: the "visionary temple" that Hilda had conceived as "over-arched by a Dome like the cloudy firmament" is finally contained in a Roman church that "has room for its cloudy pinnacles beneath the Dome." Whether this conclusion means that Saint Peter's genuinely accommodates or gradually co-opts the idea of heaven, though, remains difficult to decide.

Materiality, sensory appeal, adaptedness to human limitations, multiplicity, mediatory process, and ritual repetition: these qualities, all associated with Saint Peter's in the passage we have examined, are the qualities that characterize Catholicism in *The Marble Faun*. It is, Hawthorne writes, a faith that "marvellously adapts itself to every human need" by supplying "a multitude of external forms, in which the Spiritual may be clothed and manifested," and "many painted windows, as it were, through which the celestial sunshine, else disregarded, may make itself gloriously perceptible in visions of beauty and splendour" (344). Here, he continues, "whenever the hunger for divine nutriment came upon the soul, it could on the instant be appeased. At one or another altar, the incense was forever ascending; the mass always being performed, and carrying upward with it the devotion of such as had not words for their own prayer" (346). The convenience of Catholic worship and its adaptability to human need is further exemplified by the ubiquitous shrines, such as the ones at which Donatello stops to pray during his penitential pilgrimage, and by the array

of saints humanizing and personalizing the religion through their service as "divine auditors . . . [who] had not always been divine, but
kept, within their heavenly memories, the tender humility of a human
experience" (346). Above all, the rite of confession epitomizes Catholicism's appeal. Readily available, comfortably formalistic, infinitely repeatable, and immediately effective, it is at once a human
communication and a divine one that may take place in any language,
as if to symbolize that "there was access to the Divine Grace for every
Christian soul; there was an ear for what the overburthened heart
might have to murmur, speak in what native tongue it would" (356).

In all of these ways, Roman Catholicism offers itself to Hawthorne and his characters as an eminently habitable religious structure,
a "central home of the world." One basis of their resistance to this
offer is the suspicion that Catholicism is too easily habitable, too in-
discriminately accommodating, to serve as a spiritual home. To them,
it provides more of a way station, or a multitude of way stations, than
it does a religious origin or destination. This critique is implicit in
Hawthorne's references to the proliferation of shrines and altars in
Italy and to the spontaneous and "parenthetically devout" (295) ob-
servances that they elicit from passers-by. While the narrator deems it
"a wise and lovely sentiment, that set up the frequent shrine and
Cross, along the roadside" (298), there is the suggestion that these sites
of worship are devalued by their multiplication and that, in being so
ubiquitously at home in the world, the Church betrays its transcendental homelessness. This suggestion is a more overt and accusative
element of the novel's Protestant response to Catholic confession, a
response conveyed most vehemently in the record of Kenyon's
thoughts when he fears for the missing Hilda's safety among "a population, high and low, that . . . might throw off all care, remorse, and
memory of [evil], by kneeling a little while at the confessional, and
rising unburthened, active, elastic, and incited by fresh appetite for the
next ensuing sin" (411–12). Apart from its cynical estimation of the
Roman populace, this passage reflects a deeper apprehension about
the structure of Catholicism itself. Kenyon charges that Catholicism
promotes an understanding of human experience as cyclical and rep-

etitious, a transformative process with no ultimate term. As a religious idea, the Fall, whether fortunate or unfortunate, provides humankind with a *telos,* a point of origin and of destination along a linear spiritual journey. The critique of the rite of confession—and of Catholicism in general—in *The Marble Faun* is that it obscures or even precludes this singular spiritual journey by producing a multitude of material copies, imitations, even caricatures of it.

One of *The Marble Faun*'s most frequent and important images symbolically enacts this judgment of Catholicism's multiplicity and indirection by linking the contest between Catholic Rome and Protestant America to questions of artistic form and value. This is the image of chromatic or prismatic light, which is invariably placed in opposition to pure, unrefracted, white light. An example, cited above, is Hawthorne's use of the stained-glass church window as a figure for Catholicism itself, a religion that offers "many painted windows, as it were, through which the celestial sunshine, else disregarded, may make itself gloriously perceptible." Several pages later, Kenyon confirms the implication that such glorious perceptibility is achieved at the cost of purity, simplicity, naturalness, and truth. Saint Peter's should not have any "ordinary panes of glass," he tells Hilda. "Daylight, in its natural state, ought not to be admitted here. It should stream through a brilliant illusion of Saints and Hierarchies, and old Scriptural images, and symbolized Dogmas, purple, blue, golden, and a broad flame of scarlet. Then, it would be just such an illumination as the Catholic faith allows to its believers. But, give me—to live and die in—the pure, white light of Heaven!" Hilda, who has just succumbed to the relief of confession and senses the accusation in Kenyon's tone, replies: "I love the white light, too!" (366).

As we have seen, Hilda is persistently identified with the color white and with its symbolic associations: innocence, devotion, virginity, clarity of vision. She herself speaks of the white dress that she must wear spotless back to God, and in the language of Kenyon's proposal she virtually becomes the white light of heaven itself, the source of "white wisdom" that will be his "pole-star above" and "light of cottage-windows here below" to guide him home. The narrator, too, refers to the "white radiance of [Hilda's] soul" at a moment when it is assaulted by "a throng of torturing recollections" (385). This assault is precipitated when Kenyon tentatively suggests (several chapters before he repeats and quickly recants Miriam's theory of *felix culpa*) "what a mixture of good there may be in things evil" (383). Hilda responds unequivocally: "If there be any such dreadful mixture of good and evil as you affirm, (and which appears to me almost more shocking than pure evil,) then the good is turned to poison, not the evil to wholesomeness" (384). Given Hilda's characterization, her absolute distinction between the condition of "spotlessness" and that of being "stained with guilt" (385) is hardly remarkable. Given her vocation, though, it is significant and problematic. For the language that depicts the moral philosophy and the religious system that Hilda rejects also describes the art of painting that she practices. Painters *stain* canvases with a multitude of colors that are created by *mixture* and that allow them to mingle light and shadow in order to create brilliant illusions of reality.

In spite of her Catholic propensities, Hilda ultimately cannot reconcile or synthesize her moral and aesthetic commitments. Her desire for such a synthesis, though, is articulated in the one original artistic conception the novel accords her. Standing with Kenyon on a bridge overlooking the Tiber, Hilda muses on the whereabouts of "the seven-branched golden candlestick, the holy candlestick of the Jews" (370), which was said to have been lost in the river during the reign of Constantine. "When it is found again, and seven lights are kindled and burning in it," she tells her companion, "the whole world will gain the illumination which it needs. Would not this be an admirable idea for a mystic story, or parable, or seven-branched allegory, full of poetry, art, philosophy, and religion? It shall be called 'The Recovery of the Sacred Candlestick.' As each branch is lighted, it shall have a differently coloured lustre from the other six; and when all the seven are kindled, their radiance shall combine into the intense white light of Truth!" (371). Some future moment of revelation will bring purity out of amalgamation, unite "poetry, art, philosophy, and religion," and even encompass in its white light the dark lusters of Catholicism and of Judaism (whose significance will be examined in chapter 7). But, for the present, as Kenyon skeptically observes, it is likely that the candlestick "stuck where it fell . . . and, by this time, is imbedded thirty feet deep in the mud of the Tiber" (370).

Hilda's artistic conception is unexecuted in or by *The Marble Faun*. Transient colors and eternal whiteness remain unintegrated, and their antagonism, conceived in aesthetic terms, informs the novel's opposition of painting to sculpture. This comparison, as Hawthorne develops it, is analogous to the comparison of Catholic Rome and Protestant America. The multicolored painted canvas is contrasted with the white sculpted marble. The capacity of painting to convey action and relationship, and its material susceptibility to the effects of time, is contrasted with sculpture's effect of stability and with its permanence. The additive and artificial process of painting is contrasted with the supposedly subtractive and natural process by which a sculptor frees an original form (as the early Protestant reformers of Roman Catholicism believed they were doing) from the extraneous material that contains and obscures it. Hawthorne's paired descriptions of the sites of pictorial and sculptural production, in chapters entitled "Miriam's Studio" and "A Sculptor's Studio," exemplify the opposing associations of these mediums. Miriam works in a room that

> had the customary aspect of a painter's studio; one of those delightful spots that hardly seem to belong to the actual world, but rather to be the outward type of a poet's haunted imagination, where there are glimpses, sketches, and half-developed hints of beings and objects, grander and more beautiful than we can anywhere find in reality. The windows were closed with shutters, or deeply curtained, except one, which was partly open to a sunless portion of the sky, admitting only, from high upward, that partial light which, with its strongly marked contrast of shadow, is the first requisite towards seeing objects pictorially. (41)

The sculptor's domain, on the other hand, reflects the solidity and simplicity of his medium and his pursuit of an ideality less dependent on passionate fantasy and on the manipulation of vision than are painting's glimpses of the sublime. Presenting "a good deal the aspect, indeed, of a stone-mason's workshop," Kenyon's studio has "bare floors of brick, or plank, and plastered walls; [with] an old chair or two, or perhaps only a block of marble (containing, however, the possibility of ideal grace within it) to sit down upon" (114).

The "glimpses, sketches, and half-developed hints" of marvelous objects and beings that litter Miriam's studio suggest both the liveliness of her art and its lack of completeness and stability. These qualities neatly accord with Hawthorne's first image of Miriam herself as an elusive and illusive projection of light: "She resembled one of those images of light, which conjurors evoke and cause to shine before us, in apparent tangibility, only an arm's length beyond our grasp; we make a step in advance, expecting to seize the illusion, but find it still precisely so far out of our reach" (21). Miriam's sketches and paintings are similarly unsettled and unsettling. Ostensibly heroic portrayals of biblical women are perversely undermined by "a certain wayward quirk of her pencil" (43). Or, beginning a composition "in all earnestness," Miriam gives "the last touches in utter scorn, as it were, of the feeling which at first took such powerful possession of her hand" (43–44). Even her conventionally idealized domestic scenes are complicated, and their homely comfort resisted, by the ubiquitous presence of "a figure . . . pourtrayed [*sic*] apart" (46).

Miriam's works are inescapably self-referential, colored by her personal conflicts, desires, and history—the source, Hawthorne indicates, of their power. "Whatever technical merit they lacked, its absence was more than supplied by a warmth and passionateness, which she had the faculty of putting into her productions, and which all the world could feel. Her nature had a great deal of colour, and, in accordance with it, so likewise had her pictures" (20–21). That her pictures take their color from her nature is also their limitation. Incorporating the needs and passions they cannot transcend, these compositions are volatile *mixtures* of the ideal and the carnal. After witnessing Miriam's and Donatello's crime, Hilda perceives the same limitation and the same unholy mixture to characterize the art of the Italian masters whom she had venerated. Their Virgins and infant Christs suddenly strike her as possessing "no more mixture of the Divine than just enough to spoil them as representations of Maternity and Childhood, with which everybody's heart might have something to do" (336). The occasional image of Mary that did "excite devotional feeling," she thinks, "was probably the object of [the artist's] earthly love" (337); in this way, the old masters "deified their light and wandering affections" by "offering the features of some venal beauty to be enshrined in the holiest places" (338).

Hilda's disillusioned judgment of Renaissance religious painting is the same judgment that Kenyon later passes on Catholicism, that it deals in "canonized humanity" (458). And her loss of confidence in the moral depth and substance of such works of art, which now appear to her as "crust[s] of paint over an emptiness" (341), recalls the early depiction of Miriam as an illusory image of light. The substitution of "glowing earthliness" (337) and "external arrangement" (339) for "spiritual insight" (375) in painting prompts the narrator's bitter observation that "shallow and worldly men are among the best critics" of pictures and that "a taste for pictorial art is often no more than a polish upon the hard enamel of an artificial character" (339). It is this sense of painting's betrayed spiritual promise, moreover, that is emblematized in the earthly fate of Italy's "faded frescoes": once "radiant," their "colours are so wretchedly bedimmed—now that blotches of plaistered wall dot the frescoes all over, like a mean reality thrusting itself through life's brightest illusions—[that] the next best artist to Cimabue, or Giotto, or Ghirlandaio, or Pinturicchio, will be he that shall reverently cover their ruined master-pieces with whitewash!" (303).

Sculpture would appear to triumph over painting in the rivalry of the arts that *The Marble Faun* enacts. For Hawthorne, "marble assumes a sacred character," and its "pure, white, undecaying substance" both obliges and facilitates "the delicate evolution of spiritual, through material beauty" (135–36). As a medium, sculpture stands opposed to the wandering affections and wayward passions that painting betrays, its adulterated and perishable colors, and its mingled illusory and earthy qualities. In fact, Miriam explains her visit to Kenyon's studio as an attempt to escape from these qualities of her own art and life: "I have come to try whether there is any calm and coolness among your marbles. My own art is too nervous, too passionate, too full of agitation, for me to work at it whole days together, without intervals of repose" (116–17). Like Hawthorne, Miriam associates the cool, white, solid marble with emotional and moral, as well as physical, repose. (The other purpose of her visit to Kenyon, which I will discuss momentarily, is to share her troubling secret with him in the hope of relieving her moral agitation.) Kenyon most clearly articulates this association in the second chapter when he criticizes the statue of the dying gladiator for its failure to achieve stasis or resolution: "Flitting moments—imminent emergencies—imperceptible intervals between two breaths—ought not to be incrusted with the eternal repose of marble; in any sculptural subject, there should be a moral standstill, since there must of necessity be a physical one. Otherwise, it is like flinging a block of marble up into the air, and, by some trick of enchantment, causing it to stick there" (16).

If painting is aligned not only with Catholicism but with what might be called moral catholicity, an openness to a range of possibilities, relativities, and processes, then sculpture in *The Marble Faun* signifies a kind of fundamentalism. Kenyon's critique of the dying gladiator early establishes the link between sculpture and fulfillment, revelation, or judgment. Throughout the novel, too, sculptures provide the primary occasions for moralizing or sermonizing. "There are sermons in stones," Hilda remarks, responding to Kenyon's disquisition on Trajan's forum (151). Most often it is Kenyon, the character whom Hawthorne repeatedly calls his "man of marble," who delivers the sermons, as he does beneath the statue of the bronze pontiff in Perugia when he tells Miriam and Donatello that Heaven "recognizes your union here below," so long as it is not "for earthly bliss" (322). Kenyon's ministerial authority is reinforced by the narrator's remark that the eternality of marble confers a "religious obligation" (135) upon its molders, and that "no man should dare to touch it unless he feels within himself a certain consecration" (136). One recent critic, who reads *The Marble Faun* as a drama of the salvation of humankind in which each character plays an allegorical part, casts Kenyon as God Himself.[4] And, indeed, as an artist whose marble figures are conceptualized and modeled by him but finally produced by subordinates according to his verbal directions and without any physical labor on his part, Kenyon creates in a manner that is pointedly compared to God's. Of his work, Hawthorne writes: "His creative power has wrought it with a word" (115).

Hawthorne's "man of marble" is thus also a man of the word. An American Protestant male, devoted to "the pure, white light of Heaven" and possessed of a God-like creative power, Kenyon is a figure if not of divine authority then at least of literary authority. Criticism of *The Marble Faun* has commonly regarded him as Hawthorne's representative in the text. Yet, as an authorial presence, let alone as a godly one, Kenyon has several ironic limitations, and these limitations implicitly qualify the claims of sculpture to superiority over painting. Although he pronounces the moral of Miriam's and Donatello's dark union, Kenyon is the only one of the four main characters who—until he is trotted out to answer the readers' questions in the postscript that Hawthorne added after the book's original publication—*never knows what happens*. He neither participates in nor sees the model's murder, and no one ever tells him about it. He does not know where Hilda disappears to, nor does he participate in arranging her reappearance, and no one ever explains these events to him either. In the final chapters, his gravity, dignity, and authority are mocked and playfully assaulted during the Roman carnival (whose significance I will discuss in chapter 6), before he entreats Hilda to guide him home. Clearly, Kenyon cannot be said to possess "the master-word" here.

Kenyon almost learns the secret of Miriam's past when she comes to his studio, before the model's murder, hoping to find relief in confession "to only one human soul." She has chosen him, after viewing his sculpted Cleopatra, because, as she says, "you see far into womanhood! You receive it widely into your large view! Perhaps—perhaps—but Heaven only knows—you might understand me! Oh, let me speak!" (128). Kenyon has the right *words* for the occasion, but he invites Miriam's confession with all the "calm and coolness" of his art and with a suggestion of the physical disengagement that characterizes his relationship to his marble figures. Miriam recoils, telling him: "You are as cold and pitiless as your own marble" (129). In fact, this scene dramatically enacts the criticism to which the novel often subjects the art of sculpture—that it is cold, abstract, and inflexible, that it cannot comprehend change or respond to the immediacies of human need. Kenyon himself, studying some statues in a gallery, judges them to be artworks that derive "their vitality more from thought than passion" (390).

In contrast to painting's heat, sculpture is characterized by Miriam as the "frozen art" (17). She uses the term in contesting Kenyon's call for a "moral standstill" in art and arguing, instead, for the "scope and freedom" of temporality: "a story can be so much more fully told, in picture," she says, "and buttressed about with circumstances that give it an epoch" (17). Later, however, she extends her charge. Not only the sculptural subject, but the practice of sculpture itself—by which she means the neoclassical sculpture of Kenyon and of the mid-nineteenth-century American artists whom Hawthorne knew in Italy—is frozen in time; it may have reference to Greece and to eternity, but it has little relevance to the lives people live here and now. Kenyon ultimately detaches himself from the story and the surrounding circumstances of *The Marble Faun*'s here and now. He rejects Rome, Catholicism, and the theory of the Fortunate Fall and consigns Miriam and Donatello to their alien experience. But his decision to leave unfinished his final sculpture, the marble bust of Donatello, suggests Kenyon's partial conversion away from the aesthetic of the moral standstill. This "imperfect" work achieves no repose but rather conveys the "riddle" and "process of moral growth" (381). In contradistinction to Kenyon's avowed artistic values at the beginning of the novel, and to the values associated with both Protestantism and America throughout, this is a work in marble whose formal and moral resolution hangs suspended, up in the air.

Hawthorne's narrator concludes his description of Kenyon's unfinished marble bust of Donatello by remarking that it was the impetus for his narrative. "It was the contemplation of this imperfect portrait of Donatello that originally interested us in his history, and impelled us to elicit from Kenyon what he knew of his friend's adventures" (381). This information reinforces *The Marble Faun*'s ambivalent association of literary art both with painting and with sculpture. Here, the narrative is linked to a sculpture, but one that defies the governing principles of that medium, as Kenyon and others have articulated them. This sculpture, significantly, is called a "portrait," but it is not clear whether the narrator's interest in it lies in its suggestive incompletion or in the urge to complete it, "perfect" it, solve its riddle. To some degree, writing is conceived in *The Marble Faun* as the art that can mediate between painting and sculpture and between the opposing values that, as this chapter has shown, attach to them. Language is obviously a temporal medium, even better suited to the elaboration of story and circumstance that Miriam praises painting's ability to convey. At the same time, in its abstraction, its more intellectual than sensory production and apprehension, and its association with the idea of authority, the word is linked to sculpture. Hawthorne reinforces this link by the references that we have noted to Kenyon's creation with a word and to sermons in stones, and by several allusions to engraving—a process that evokes both writing and sculpting and that, at least in the instance when the murder Hilda observes is said to "grave itself in the eternal adamant" (171), seems to allude to sacred words cast in stone.

From the outset of his career as a novelist, Hawthorne had defined his art as a form of mediation. In the preface to *The Scarlet Letter,* in his most famous definition of romance, he holds his fiction to be "a neutral territory, somewhere between the real world and fairyland, where the Actual and the Imaginary may meet, and each imbue itself with the nature of the other" (*CE,* 1:36). This account of romance is echoed in the characterization of the faun of Praxiteles as "neither man nor animal, and yet no monster, but a being in whom both races meet, on friendly ground!" (10). Yet, in *The Marble Faun,* the "neutral territory" or "friendly ground" of romance is more aptly described as a battlefield on which "the Actual" and "the Imaginary" bleed confusedly into each other, the conceptual distinction between them—like the meaning of "home" discussed earlier in this chapter—having become unstable. As I have suggested, Hawthorne, in his mid-fifties and living abroad, was both fascinated and deeply threatened by the instability of his lifelong conceptual categories. The fascination is reflected in *The Marble Faun*'s radical and volatile mixtures of supposed opposites; the threat is reflected in its reactionary efforts to restore order through polarization, to undo these mixtures and reassert stark distinctions between their elements by idealizing one paired term and degrading the other. Accordingly, the novel's representation of literary art itself—poetry, romance—is polarized. At one moment it is idealized, at another degraded, and only intermittently is it seen to exercise mediatory powers.

Hawthorne's polarized image of his own art is illustrated by a pair of remarks that associate poetry (which is repeatedly linked to romance here) first with sculpture and idealization, then with painting and degradation. About Praxiteles' faun, Hawthorne observes: "Only a sculptor of the finest imagination, the most delicate taste, the sweetest feeling, and the rarest artistic skill—in a word, a sculptor and a poet too—could have first dreamed of a faun in this guise, and then have succeeded in imprisoning the sportive and frisky thing, in marble" (10). Later, describing a "picturesquely time-stained" Italian village, he comments: "An artist, it is true, might often thank his stars for those old houses. . . . But there is reason to suspect that a people are waning to decay and ruin, the moment that their life becomes fascinating either in the poet's imagination or the painter's eye" (296). This latter passage echoes the central paragraph of Hawthorne's preface to *The Marble Faun*, a paragraph in which he effectively forfeits the earlier claim of his art to mediate between the Actual and the Imaginary.

> Italy, as the site of his Romance, was chiefly valuable to him as affording a sort of poetic or fairy precinct, where actualities would not be so terribly insisted upon, as they are, and must needs be, in America. No author, without a trial, can conceive of the difficulty of writing a Romance about a country where there is no shadow,

no antiquity, no mystery, no picturesque and gloomy wrong, nor anything but a common-place prosperity, in broad and simple daylight, as is happily the case with my dear native land. It will be very long, I trust, before romance-writers may find congenial and easily handled themes either in the annals of our stalwart Republic, or in any characteristic and probable events of our individual lives. Romance and poetry, like ivy, lichens, and wall-flowers, need Ruin to make them grow. (3)

Here, romance is depicted as an art that can exist, somewhat contradictorily, only in a region of transcendence (a "poetic or fairy precinct") and in an atmosphere of ruin. In neither case does it engage American "actualities." Hawthorne literally exiles it from America in this passage and ignores or forgets the fact that he himself has previously published three romances that take their themes from American history and the events of American life. In chapter 7 I will discuss the implications of Hawthorne's representation of America, virtually on the eve of the Civil War, as a place of "common-place prosperity" without "shadow" or "gloomy wrong." But, for the moment, we may observe in this passage Hawthorne's uneasy suspicion that the practice of his art is somehow un-American. He has an impulse to criticize the limitations on imagination and experience that his vision of American life imposes ("so terribly insisted upon") but immediately squelches it by a pledge of allegiance to that vision ("and must needs be"). Thus, the preface strongly suggests that Hawthorne's physical and emotional return to the "broad and simple daylight" of his "dear native land" is predicated, as Hilda's and Kenyon's return is, upon the repudiation of art.

Richard Brodhead also argues that *The Marble Faun* bears the signs of a psychological repudiation of literary practice, or a growing alienation from "fiction's ground of motivation," that would manifest itself, after Hawthorne's return to America, in his inability to complete another romance (Brodhead, 69). Brodhead attributes this failure to a rift between the work of producing literary art and the idea of a work of art that Hawthorne had come to hold by the time he began to write *The Marble Faun*. This rift, or opposition, between a human process and an idealized product is akin to the oppositions, of painting to sculpture and of Catholicism to Protestantism, with which this chapter has been concerned. For Brodhead, though, the self-division of *The Marble Faun* is best explained as a consequence of the dramatic "reorganization . . . of the category of the literary and of literature's place in the culture" that took place in America during the 1850s. During Hawthorne's eight-year literary sabbatical, the managers of American culture—publishers, magazine editors, prominent critics—had effectively "split writing into separate categories of literary and popular, hierarchically related as high and low," and "refashioned the social status of authorship—creating a new, inferior status for the popular writer, but also building for certain literary writers a greatly augmented stature, as transcendent achievers and national treasures" (Brodhead, 70). Hawthorne was advanced—and accepted his new status—as one of the nation's principal literary treasures. But the effect of this canonization, this monumentalization, of a still living writer, Brodhead suggests, was to incapacitate him for writing. Hawthorne became, to play on a phrase of Miriam's quoted above, a kind of "frozen artist"—compelled by his own monumental stature to resist rather than welcome development or change, and committed by his role as representative of an insecurely established high culture to police the moral and aesthetic border between the impure and the pure, the merely human and the divine. Hawthorne struggles with this role in his last novel, but ultimately—like Miriam struggling to escape the identity and the fate that she has been assigned—he can only fulfill it.

Brodhead shows that the European cultural environment of *The Marble Faun*, in which art "exists primarily as completed artifact, something already made and already designated as of classic value," may be seen to mirror a mid-nineteenth-century American cultural environment "in which art has been strongly reidentified not with the work of making but with a canon of masters and masterpieces" (Brodhead, 72–73). One quality that these environments share is that, in both, the authority of classic artifacts and canonical art is a male authority. In fact, the reorganization of American literature that Brodhead describes was powerfully motivated by the desire to promote a group of literary *masters* as clearly distinct from the popular women writers of the day, and to establish an exalted category of literary *masterpieces* as clearly superior to the productions of what Hawthorne once called this "damned mob of scribbling women" (*CE,* 17:304). This historical context suggests another set of terms relevant to the struggles and polarities of *The Marble Faun.* The novel we have approached in terms of competing mythic structures, competing working models of art, and the competing pressures of "Catholic propensities" and Puritan heritage, must now be examined as a work shaped and misshapen by its sexual politics.

6

The Rise of Women

In a recent book entitled *Nathaniel Hawthorne and the Romance of the Orient*, Luther S. Luedtke has documented Hawthorne's "unexpectedly extensive readings of voyages, travels, histories, and imaginative literature of the East" and has examined his lifelong interest in, and literary uses of, the idea of the Orient.[1] This interest began early in Hawthorne's childhood and had a personal source in the logbooks that detailed the East India voyages of his father, a captain of a merchant ship who died at sea when his son was three years old. As Luedtke points out, however, a fascination with the Orient in a literate young American of Hawthorne's time was hardly a personal idiosyncrasy. "Orientalism," he writes, "pervad[ed] the literature of the United States, especially during the development of nineteenth-century Romanticism" (Luedtke, xxi). Works such as *The Arabian Nights Entertainment* (1705–1708) and Thomas Moore's *Lalla Rookh: An Eastern Romance* (1817) were best-sellers in the early republic. A bit later, Emerson, Thoreau, and the other American Transcendentalists were developing a philosophy based in part on their readings of Indian mythology and Persian poetry; Irving, Poe, and many others were filling American magazines with Oriental tales; and literary pilgrims to

70

the Holy Land (a class that would include Mark Twain and Hawthorne's friends George William Curtis and Herman Melville) were returning with stories, impressions, and exotica collected from their travels (Luedtke, xxi).

The Orient served the aesthetic, social, and psychological purposes of Hawthorne's contemporaries as it has served the West from the Middle Ages through the Vietnam War: as an image of otherness, or of "the Other." It represents the allure and the threat of the unknown, the strange, the unhomelike, and the qualities with which it is identified are those that the dominant culture of the West contemplates with mingled desire, fear, and condescension. The Occident defines itself against the Orient through a series of invented antitheses: Western clarity against Eastern mystery; Western discipline and practicality against Eastern luxuriance; Western intellect against Eastern sensuality; Western virtue and order against disorderly Eastern vice. These qualities of the cultural and geographical Other are generally the same ones that a male-dominated society assigns to the sexual Other—woman. Thus, the literature and art of that society might draw on the associations of the Orient to give color and force to its constructions of the female, and vice versa.

Hawthorne's dark-haired, knowledge-stained women, Luedtke observes, all possess "Oriental" qualities. Hester Prynne betrays a "rich, voluptuous . . . Oriental characteristic—a taste for the gorgeously beautiful" (*CE*, 1:83); sensual, aggressive Zenobia in *The Blithedale Romance* bears the name of the Syrian queen who was defeated by the Roman emperor Aurelian in A.D. 272 and brought captive to Rome; and Miriam's face is described as having "a certain rich Oriental character" (22). Hawthorne shared with some of the most prominent American sculptors of his day this tendency to orientalize rebellious and provocative female figures. Hiram Powers's nudes, *Eve Tempted* and *The Greek Slave*, aroused admiration, controversy, and, doubtless, some libidos during their international exhibition tours. And William Wetmore Story, whose studio Hawthorne visited often in Rome, produced his *Cleopatra* and began *The Libyan Sybil* during Hawthorne's stay and went on to sculpt the nudes *Salome* and *Delilah*.

"Competing images of female sovereignty and subjugation," Luedtke reports, "became increasingly commonplace in Western culture from the 1830s onwards" (Luedtke, 196). American neoclassical sculpture, in particular, often took up this competition and gave it a formal resolution. For in works such as the ones cited by Powers and Story, "the male artist eventually immobilizes the passionate Oriental female in stone" (Luedtke, 196–97).

Hawthorne understood the captivity and immobilization of the female to be a prime function on these statues. This is evident in his description of Kenyon's *Cleopatra* and of Miriam's response to it. Kenyon's sculpture, which Hawthorne acknowledges in his preface to be modeled on Story's, has succeeded in capturing "all Cleopatra—fierce, voluptuous, passionate, tender, wicked, terrible, and full of poisonous and rapturous enchantment" (127). Yet, in it she has "relinquished all activity" and sits in a repose "as complete as if she were never to stir hand or foot again," a "marvellous repose— . . . the repose of despair" (126). Miriam's first reaction reinforces the suggestion that Kenyon's artistic accomplishment is a kind of military and sexual conquest, a neutralization or domestication of Cleopatra's power and passion: "Tell me, did she never try—even while you were creating her—to overcome you with her fury, or her love? Were you not afraid to touch her, as she grew more and more towards hot life, beneath your hand?" (127). Through the conversation that follows, Hawthorne intimates that Miriam herself may have been the model for "the womanhood" that Kenyon has embodied in Cleopatra, a type of womanhood that he could have "never found . . . in [his] gentle Hilda" (127). This suggestion is, in fact, borne out by the interesting relationship between the statue of Cleopatra and the self-portrait by Miriam that is described earlier. Kenyon's work immobilizes the volatile beauty, neutralizes her powers of enchantment, and subdues her "beneath [his] hand." It is the Cleopatra who was conquered by Octavius Caesar. But Miriam's work evokes nothing so much as the Cleopatra who made a conquest of, and would not be domesticated by, Mark Antony: "There appeared the portrait of a beautiful woman, such as one sees only two or three, if even so many, in all a lifetime; so beautiful, that she seemed to get into your consciousness and memory, and could never afterwards be shut out, but haunted your dreams, for pleasure or for pain; holding your inner realm as a conquered territory, though without deigning to make herself at home there" (47–48).

The domestic ideology of the nineteenth-century American middle class was designed to ensure that women "made themselves at home" in the places assigned to them in the male imagination and the patriarchal family. At a time when images and standards of masculine behavior were shifting and insecure, and when many men had come to doubt their sovereignty over their own fates and fortunes, fathers and husbands could at least claim and enforce their sovereignty over the women in their homes. Thus, the society invested women with a thoroughgoing "otherness," yet sought to contain any autonomy, and to eliminate any danger or mystery, that this status might entail.

The domestication of women was not solely a matter of inculcating the attitudes that a woman only achieved her proper identity through her relationship to a man, and that a nonproductive woman was a happy symbol of the ability of the man of the house to provide for her every need. It was, as Carroll Smith-Rosenberg demonstrates in her book *Disorderly Conduct: Visions of Gender in Victorian America,* a systematic effort in which many of the nation's most pervasive and powerful institutions—such as government, medicine, and the law—played large roles. Laws regulating women's inheritance and property rights limited their prospects for economic independence. Women's bodies, as well, were brought under the legal and medical control of men. Abortion, which had been legal in the United States throughout its history and was often performed relatively safely by skilled women practitioners, began to be criminalized by state legislatures in the 1840s and 1850s. At the same time, a newly centralized and professionalized medical community (purged of "irregular," country-trained, homeopathic women doctors) relentlessly publicized its "scientific" findings about the female body. Those findings held that every aspect of a woman's life was "driven by the tidal currents of her cyclical reproductive system," and that, these currents being unclean, the female body was a veritable haven of disease.[2] Women also were creatures of limited vitality, who, particularly during the early years of puberty, needed all the energy they had for the healthy development of their reproductive organs. Any excessive exertion of the body, the mind, or the emotions, and especially any "unfeminine" occupations, stimulations, or assertions of will, during these years would lead to physical and mental collapse. Some physicians, Smith-Rosenberg reports, went so far as to advocate that women "subject to . . . excessive menstrual influence . . . should, for their own good and that of society, be incarcerated for the length of their menstruating years" (Smith-Rosenberg, 191). So effectively did this prevailing medical and social ethos degrade female biological processes that many ashamed mothers could not bring themselves to speak of menstruation to their daughters, thus ensuring that the first experience of menstrual blood for these young women would be one of helplessness and terror.

The degradation of female sexuality in nineteenth-century America was one of two opposing cultural operations that were joined together in a kind of dialectical synthesis. The other was the idealization of the woman whose sexual and social identity was completely invested in the patriarchal family. A woman could turn the curse of her "otherness" into a blessing for herself and society by domesticating herself and becoming enshrined as the angel of the home, which, women were repeatedly told, was their natural and healthy sphere, the site not of their restriction but of their true freedom and power. Moreover, the same medical experts who held female personality to be dominated by the sex organs rather contradictorily asserted (in direct opposition to prevailing medical opinion earlier in the century) that normal women tended toward sexual frigidity, that their only natural interest in sex was reproduction (Smith-Rosenberg, 23). Thus, in charting the approved course of female redemption and sanctification, male representatives of cultural authority sought, as Smith-Rosenberg suggestively puts it, "to wash the menstrual blood white in the rhetorical spirituality of marriage and motherhood" (Smith-Rosenberg, 189).

For the reader of *The Marble Faun*, the depiction of the idealized woman presented above can hardly fail to conjure up the image of Hilda. It is Hilda who is literally redeemed, or ransomed, in exchange for her degraded "sister" Miriam. And, in the logic of the novel's conclusion, this redemption symbolically enacts and endorses the triumph of American domestic ideology. To return home and marry Kenyon is ultimately the only way for Hilda to wash clean the spot on her consciousness (repeatedly imaged as a bloodstain on her white robe) that she has incurred while wandering freely in Rome at midnight. As if to punctuate this point, Miriam appears to Kenyon and Hilda an instant after they have become engaged, but now, Hawthorne writes, it is "as if Miriam stood on the other side of a fathomless abyss" (461). Kenyon's own image of the life he offers Hilda is a distillation of domestic ideology: he hopes "to take this shy, frank, and innocently fearless creature, captive, and imprison her in his heart, and make her sensible of a wider freedom, there, than in all the world besides" (395). The "daughter of the Puritans" who becomes captivated by "the Old Masters" and is later arrested by Church Fathers happily ends her career imprisoned in her husband's heart and home. The task of tending the Virgin's flame is replaced by that of keeping the home fires burning; the small Protestant contributor to the Catholic cult of the Virgin assumes her own place as the idol in the American cult of true womanhood.

In chapter 4, we examined the ethical and aesthetic dimensions of the choice between what the novel characterizes as Roman and American, or Catholic and Protestant, orientations toward experience. But the parallels and repetitions between the various phases of Hilda's experience suggest that, for a woman, the apparent choice may be no choice at all. *The Marble Faun* may be read, then, as a work built around the threat (embodied in Miriam) and the containment (effected, in different ways, upon both Hilda and Miriam) of the female Other. Such a reading, as I have shown, is firmly anchored in the sexual politics of Hawthorne's class and culture. To develop it and evaluate its significance, though, requires that we contextualize it more specifically in relation to Hawthorne's earlier work and to his personal history and family situation.

A reader of Hawthorne can scarcely escape noticing that his fiction is full of ambivalent representations of women. Long before feminist critics of the 1960s and 1970s began to focus attention on images of women in classic American literature, many of the religious and psychological interpretations of Hawthorne that had been made centered on his polarization of dark and fair women characters. In this conventional opposition, the dark lady is aligned with sexuality, lawlessness, and knowledge or guilt, and the fair lady with virgin modesty, lawfulness, and innocence. For moralists, Hawthorne's triumphant fair ladies signaled his commitment to Christian virtues and social conservatism; for romantics and psychologists, the tragic and compelling dark ladies signaled his underlying radicalism or his Victorian prurience and sexual guilt.

This debate anticipated a more recent division among feminist critics: some see a misogynist Hawthorne, others see a feminist Hawthorne. The misogynist uses women as symbolic tokens, subordinating their humanity to the schematic demands of his fiction and punishing any female character who challenges these demands or threatens the social order that they reflect. He is also the man who, outside of his fiction, repeatedly and patronizingly commends women to their "proper sphere" as he villifies the "damned mob of scribbling women" who are his literary competitors and deplores the "false liberality, which mistakes the strong division-lines of Nature for arbitrary distinctions."[3] The feminist, on the other hand, depicts more forcefully than any male writer of his time the victimization of superior women by a patriarchal society. In fact, in the view of Nina Baym, the critic who has made the strongest case for Hawthorne's feminism, women in his fiction regularly possess "desirable and valuable qualities lacking in the male protagonist."[4]

The most famous and most fully realized woman in Hawthorne's fiction, and the one whom readers typically have found most interesting and attractive, is, of course, Hester Pyrnne. Hester's treatment in *The Scarlet Letter,* however, can be construed to support the argument for Hawthorne's misogyny as well as the argument for his feminism. Hester clearly possesses appealing qualities of character that are lacking in Arthur Dimmesdale, and most readers have felt that the affective power of the novel is centered in her story rather than in his. But Hester is clearly punished, too, for her challenge to the social order, first by the imposition of the scarlet letter, and then again by Dimmesdale's choice of self-revelation and a solitary death over her plan, to which he had earlier assented, for them to leave the Puritan community together. In the novel's second to last paragraph, Hester is said to assure all the unhappy women who come to her for comfort and counsel "that, at some brighter period, when the world should have grown ripe for it, in Heaven's own time, a new truth would be revealed, in order to establish the whole relation between man and woman on a surer ground of mutual happiness" (*CE*, 1:263). Hawthorne may allow Hester a vision of the "new truth" of sexual equality here, but if so, his own commitment to and comprehension of such a vision remains suspect. For the passage goes on to characterize it as a "divine and mysterious truth," rather than a plain social and moral necessity, and to assert "the impossibility" that "a woman stained with sin, bowed down with shame, or even burdened with a life-long sorrow" could ever be its prophet. The role of "angel and apostle of the coming revelation," Hawthorne writes, is reserved for a woman who is unimpeachably "lofty" and "pure" (*CE*, 1:263). Hawthorne's self-representations in "The Custom-House," his preface to *The Scarlet Letter*, offer little clarification of the novel's conscious sexual politics. In introducing his tale about the punishment of a socially "deviant" woman, he mentions that his prominent Puritan ancestors distinguished themselves by punishing such women (witches and Quakers) and remarks that "strong traits of their nature have intertwined themselves with mine" (*CE*, 1:10). Yet, later in the preface, he identifies with the transgressing woman rather than with the chastising patriarchy. "Discovering" Hester Prynne's faded scarlet letter in the custom-house storeroom, he places it on his own breast and experiences "a sensation not altogether physical, yet almost so, as of burning heat; and as if the letter were not of red cloth, but red-hot iron" (*CE*, 1:32).

In the opening paragraph of "The Custom-House," Hawthorne announces that his essay will indulge an "autobiographical impulse" but, at the same time, promises to "keep the inmost Me behind its veil" (*CE*, 1:4). A writer inescapably trades in self-expression, however mediated or filtered by the particular form and subject matter of his work. But generations of readers have observed that Hawthorne takes peculiar and elaborate care not to express himself openly, not to allow his own feelings and beliefs to be securely located in his fiction. Hawthorne's family and friends often made the same observation of his social habits. As his sister Elizabeth remarked to his son Julian, after Hawthorne's death, "Your father kept his very existence a secret, as far as possible."[5] One way in which Hawthorne expressed himself as a writer while concealing his "inmost Me" was by presenting conflicting and fragmentary self-representations in all of the fictional characters he created. *The Scarlet Letter,* for instance, has been persuasively interpreted by critics who identify Hawthorne with each of the four principals—Hester, Dimmesdale, Chillingworth, and Pearl. Hawthorne himself suggests, in the preface to his 1851 collection of tales, *The Snow Image,* that his identity is multiply invested and multiply veiled. An author's introductory statements, along with his "external habits" and the details of his life, "hide the man, instead of displaying him," he writes. "You must make quite another kind of inquest, and look through the whole range of his fictitious characters, good and evil, in order to detect any of his essential traits" (*CE,* 11:4). Hawthorne writes "good and evil" here, but he implies, and might more revealingly have written, "male and female." Indeed, once we recognize that female characters throughout his fiction embody many of his own "essential traits," we gain a crucial insight into his habit of self-concealment or disguise. This recognition also helps explain Hawthorne's uneasy mixture of misogyny and feminism and offers us a new critical transformation of *The Marble Faun.*

Hawthorne's insistence on the "strong division-lines of Nature" that distinguish men from women belies the fact that, for him personally, these lines were blurred. There is significant biographical and literary evidence that, from an early age, Hawthorne was pulled between the conventionally defined male and female gender roles, and that he experienced his gender identity as an ambiguous and conflicted one. As Gloria Erlich has argued, in a fine study entitled *Family Themes and Hawthorne's Fiction,* Hawthorne's childhood was shaped by a longing for his dead father and by the overbearing authority of a father *figure*, his uncle, Robert Manning. Another of Hawthorne's most insightful psychological critics, T. Walter Herbert, suggests in his forthcoming *Shamans of Domesticity: The Hawthornes and the Making of the Middle-Class Family* that this inexpressible and, hence, unresolved grief for the scarcely remembered Nathaniel Hathorne (the writer himself later added the *w* to the family name) produced in Hawthorne a personality structure that, throughout his life, was perceived by himself and others as "a 'masculine' identity shielding a 'feminine' inwardness."[6] Erlich, focusing more closely on Robert Manning's presence than on Nathaniel Hathorne's absence, shows how the young Hawthorne experienced that presence as at once exemplary, reproachful, and "tinged with . . . eros."[7]

Manning was a virile, practical, successful, and outgoing man of business whose affection Hawthorne both needed and needed to resist. For a number of psychological and circumstantial reasons, Hawthorne could not easily accept Uncle Robert's authority over him or identify with his uncle without feeling as if he were betraying his real father and losing his native identity. Moreover, it is likely that, because Robert Manning was not his father, Hawthorne experienced his desire for intimacy with him—what Herbert calls his "desperate yearning for male nurture"—as an unnatural one. In more immediately obvious ways, too, his guardian's nurture and model of masculinity divided Hawthorne against himself. His mother and sisters moved to a family farm in Raymond, Maine, when Hawthorne was thirteen, leaving him in Salem under the care of his Uncle Robert, whose bed he shared into his seventeenth year and with whom he lived until he went to college. Hawthorne longed to be with the women of his family, living in what he once termed "a second garden of Eden" (*CE*, 15:150) and reading and writing according to his pleasure, rather than in the town, preparing in school, and under the practical tutelage of his uncle, to be a man. Thus, conflicting impulses to identify with Robert Manning, to passively submit to his authority and appeal, and to rebel against him generated in Hawthorne a deep sense of sexual irresolution. Literature afforded him one means of escape, both from Uncle Robert and from his own confusing feelings. In his adolescence, Hawthorne came to associate reading and writing literature not only with guilty rebellion against the demands of masculine identity but with escape from those demands into a sphere customarily inhabited by women. It was an association he carried into his adulthood and his professional life.

In his memoirs, Julian Hawthorne wrote: "My father was two men, one sympathetic and intuitional, the other critical and logical."[8] Almost without exception, Hawthorne's literary friends shared and expressed the perception of his "double sensibility" (Erlich, 124), which they described as an amalgam of male and female qualities. James Russell Lowell's "A Fable for Critics" offered a public, verse rendition of this judgment:

> When Nature was shaping him, clay was not granted
> For making so full-sized a man as she wanted,
> So, to fill out her model, a little she spared
> From some finer-grained stuff for a woman prepared,
> And she could not have hit a more excellent plan
> For making him fully and perfectly man.

The transcendentalist and early feminist, Margaret Fuller, to whom Hawthorne was less kind, praised him in similar terms upon hearing of his engagement to Sophia Peabody: "I think there will be great happiness; for if ever I saw a man who combined delicate tenderness to understand the heart of a woman, with quiet depth and manliness enough to satisfy her, it is Mr. Hawthorne" (Wagenknecht, 17–18).

Hawthorne also recognized the "feminine" elements of his own character, including not only the delicate sensibility remarked by his acquaintances but also a tendency toward passive dependence and a simultaneous attraction to and repulsion from figures of male authority and activities associated with the exercise or gratification of masculine force and appetites. Such ambivalence is repeatedly displayed in Hawthorne's public and private commentary on his own work. In his sketch "The Old Manse" and elsewhere in his early works, he depicts his tales and essays as "blossoms" and extols their fragile beauty as he scorns their failure to yield manly fruit. He is drawn to the myth of Pandora, which he retells as "a story of what nobody but myself ever dreamed of—a Paradise of children" (and it is important to note that almost half of Hawthorne's published fiction consists of children's stories), but he also regularly condemns his own implicitly effeminate childishness (*CE*, 7:63). Hawthorne most directly and suggestively confesses his "double sensibility," though, in a letter to his mother in Maine written shortly before he entered college. "Oh how I wish I was again with you, with nothing to do but go agunning. But the happiest days of my life are gone. Why was I not a girl that I might have been pinned all my life to my mother's apron" (*CE*, 15:117). The attractions of going "agunning" and of being a girl, asserted here in such close proximity, express a sexual tension that would make its way, in various forms, into Hawthorne's fiction.

The early tale "Passages from a Relinquished Work" vividly conveys the sexual tension that particularly attended Hawthorne's choice to be a writer and storyteller. As our brief biographical account has indicated, reading and writing literature were psychologically linked for Hawthorne with images of femininity, childhood, and escape or exile from the province of the father. In Hawthorne's tale, the first-person narrator defies the authority of his guardian, Parson Thump-cushion—one of a number of fictional incarnations of Robert Manning—by remaining resolutely "aloof from the regular business of life" (*CE*, 10:407) and, at last, setting off to be an itinerant storyteller. From the first sentence, in which it is stipulated that the Parson made "no distinction" between the narrator and the three natural sons who became "respectable men, and well settled in life" (*CE*, 10:405), there is a hint that the narrator's solitary rebellion involves some deviation from the sexual norm. "He could neither change the nature that God gave me, nor adapt his own inflexible mind to my peculiar character," the narrator states, absolving his guardian of responsibility for the "misfortunes" of his life (*CE*, 10:406). But no account of misfortunes follows. Hawthorne's tale, in fact, outlines the storyteller's rise to professional success—yet this very success is somehow shameful. The nature of its shamefulness may be gleaned from the narrator's explanation of his initial reluctance to begin his literary occupation: "A slight tremor seized me, whenever I thought of relinquishing the immunities of a private character, and giving every man, and for money, too, the right which no man yet possessed, of treating me with open scorn" (*CE*, 10:415). This language—hesitant, frightened, and concerned with the giving up of immunities and the selling of something private to men, who would have a right to be openly scornful once they had bought it—suggests nothing so much as the last resistance of a young *woman* on the point of not only sacrificing her virginity but initiating a career in prostitution.

Appropriately, the narrator consummates his professional ambition several pages later in a tavern. Emboldened by the alias he has assumed, and by a conversation with a young person "of doubtful sex" (*CE*, 10:419), he recites the story "Mr. Higginbotham's Catastrophe" (another of Hawthorne's own tales) to an audience that rolls on the floor with delight. But as he leaves the stage, he is handed a letter from his guardian, uncannily "directed to [his] assumed name" (*CE*, 10:420). The narrator cannot bring himself to read this letter. But his conviction that it contains an expression of "paternal wisdom, and love, and reconciliation" evokes a powerful response in him: he envisions "the puritanic figure of my guardian, standing among the fripperies of the theatre, and pointing to the players,—the fantastic and effeminate men, the painted women, the giddy girl in boy's clothes, merrier than modest,—pointing to these with solemn ridicule, and eyeing me with stern rebuke." Although unable to return home, he flees the scene of his triumph oppressed with a sense of "the guilt and madness of [his] life" (*CE*, 10:421).

In "Passages from a Relinquished Work," it is the narrator's association of his life as a storyteller with sexual ambiguity that prompts his feelings of guilt and madness. Twenty years later, with a "mob of scribbling women" as his colleagues and competitors, Hawthorne remained plagued by the same anxiety that his literary preoccupations and his masculinity were somehow incompatible. My argument here is that writing and sexual transgression or deviance were intimately connected in Hawthorne's mind. This connection was too deeply rooted in his psyche for him to reject it or even to be fully aware of it.

But it manifested itself in his repeated association of literature—both literature written by women and literature written by himself—with the shameful revelation or illicit display of female sexuality. The poems of Julia Ward Howe were "admirable," Hawthorne remarked to his publisher in 1854, "but the devil must be in the woman to publish them. . . . What a strange propensity it is in these scribbling women to make a show of their hearts, as well as their heads, upon your counter, for anybody to pry into that chooses!" (*CE*, 17:177). A new publication by another popular literary woman prompted him to write Sophia: "I wonder she did not think it necessary to be brought to bed in public, or, at least, in presence of a committee of the subscribers. My dearest, I cannot enough thank God that, with a higher and deeper intellect than any other woman, thou hast never—forgive me the bare idea!—prostituted thyself to the public, as that woman has, and as a thousand others do" (*CE*, 17:457). This is not simply the voice of Victorian prudery or chauvinism. What so unsettled Hawthorne was not the idea that writing sexually exposed women but that women sexually exposed writing—that they revealed, in other words, his profession's, and his own, essential femininity.

For 13 years after his return from college, Hawthorne withdrew to the Salem house of his mother and sisters (they had moved back from Maine). He had wagered with his college friend, Jonathan Cilley, that he would not marry within a dozen years of graduation but would devote himself exclusively to literature. Writing, during these years, thus became Hawthorne's veil, the justification of his decision to remain "aloof from the regular business of life" and the sign of his nunlike marriage to the strange ideal of Art. In 1837 Hawthorne published under his own name a selection of his sketches and stories that had appeared anonymously in magazines during his seclusion. The critical, if not popular, success of *Twice-Told Tales*, and the public fact of his authorship, helped bring him out into society, and soon he was engaged to be married to Sophia Peabody. Suddenly, the man who had lived principally in his imagination—and who had always understood the life of the imagination to be one of rebellion against or escape from conventional adult manhood—faced conventional responsibilities. He was to be a husband and had to be a breadwinner. Throughout his long engagement and the early years of his marriage, Hawthorne attempted to reconcile his imaginative needs and ambitions with the practical necessities of his life. By the middle 1840s, however, it had become obvious that he could not support his family by writing. Accepting a political appointment in the Salem customhouse, Hawthorne suspended his literary efforts. Like Parson Thumpcushion's natural and obedient sons, he was becoming "respectable" and "well settled," a man whose workplace symbolized the province of "regular business" and of the fathers. Moreover, he was now a father himself.

A part of Hawthorne, the middle-aged family man and customhouse surveyor, scorned Hawthorne the failed storyteller, the effeminate dreamer who would not grow up. A part of Hawthorne, in other words, had finally become the man that Parson Thumpcushion or Robert Manning was. But even as he appeared to have "relinquished" literary work in the late 1840s, he continued to think of himself as a writer. Hawthorne harbored his rebellious, imaginative energies deep within, but he also preserved them, during these years, by transferring them to another being, a child, in whom he could see them outwardly reflected. That child was his daughter Una. Una was marked from birth as a representative of the world of imagination and romance when her father named her after the heroine of Spenser's *The Faerie Queene*. The name troubled family and friends, one of whom wrote to Hawthorne that it should be "rather kept and hallowed in the holy crypts of the mind, than brought into the garish light of common day" (*Works*, 14:276). The remark proved prophetic. Una would remain throughout her life a product and a prisoner of Hawthorne's imagination rather than an inhabitant of the common day.

Every member of the Hawthorne family remarked on the infant Una's "immense . . . force" (*Works*, 14:306) and on her physical and temperamental likeness to her father. Hawthorne's wife and son also testified to his special and intense affection for her. This affection could be frank and spontaneous, but from the beginning it included an obsessive quality and was mingled with resistance and feelings of guilt that Hawthorne projected onto Una's character. Hawthorne's complex response to his daughter was a product of his half-conscious idea that she embodied his own repressed, yet cherished, creative life, that she represented his richly imaginative but irresponsible and some-how deviant art. He closely recorded her behavior and early speech in notebooks and invariably described her in the language of the imagi-nation. (By contrast, he described his son Julian in mundane, practical terms.) "There is something that almost frightens me about the child," he observes in one journal entry about the five-year-old Una. "I now and then catch an aspect of her, in which I cannot believe her to be my own human child, but a spirit strangely mingled with good and evil, haunting the house where I dwell. The little boy is always the same child, and never varies in his relation to me." What frightened Hawthorne about the unpredictability of his daughter's relationship to him was its reflection of his own internal inconsistency. In his notes on Una, he is repeatedly entranced and appalled by what he calls her "manifestations," her ability to pass "from one character to another, male and female, youth, age, or infancy . . . like the little flames that quiver and dance at the top of a coal grate" (*CE*, 8:411). This image of Una is very similar to the images of the art of romance, or of the romancer's power to distribute himself among a variety of characters, that are scattered throughout Hawthorne's writing. And it is followed by a reaction against the illusoriness and instability that Hawthorne also frequently associated with his own art: it is useless to seek Una's "real soul," he pronounces, "for, before the establishment of princi-ples, what is character but the series and successions of moods?" (*CE*, 8:413).

In reading these characterizations of Una, we may be struck by how nearly they anticipate some of the depictions of the art and reli-gion of Rome—and especially some of the images of Miriam—in *The Marble Faun*, written almost a decade later. Una was, in Hawthorne's mind, a figure who mingled good and evil and who *haunted* his house, rather than domesticating herself in it as his "own human child." She was associated, like the Catholic Church, with "series and succes-sions" that disguised the "real soul" or deferred its establishment. Like

Miriam's paintings, she displayed restlessness and unpredictability and resisted a moral standstill. And, like Miriam herself, who is compared to "one of those images of light, which conjurors evoke," Una was likened by her father to the play of a flame that cannot be arrested.

In fact, Una was prominently on her father's mind during the composition of *The Marble Faun*. Hawthorne had begun to withdraw from his daughter several years before, during his service as American consul in Liverpool and during her passage into adolescence. For her part, Una had gone through a brief period of anger and rebellion. But she continued to idolize her father, and, as he had done at the same age, she found comfort and refuge in voracious reading. In England, Una also developed a sudden interest in religious forms and ceremonies. This interest distressed Hawthorne, who depicted it, intriguingly, as a desire to get unnaturally close to the heavenly Father. At some level, his comment suggests, he understood this desire to be motivated by Una's longing to regain her closeness to her earthly father: "Shall the whole sky be the dome of her cathedral? or must she compress the Deity into a narrow space, for the purpose of getting at him more readily?"[9] Una's "Catholic propensities" only increased in Rome, stimulated by the Renaissance art that she quickly came to adore. Hawthorne wrote in his notebook: "We shall have done the child no good office, in bringing her here, if the rest of her life is to be a dream of this 'city of the soul,' and an unsatisfied yearning to come back" (*CE*, 14:230). But he was to have greater cause for guilt than this in Rome's effect on Una.

In October 1858, apparently while sketching outdoors near the Palace of the Caesars, 14-year-old Una contracted malaria. For months she lay seriously ill; at one point the doctor told her mother that he doubted she could live another 12 hours. On 25 October Hawthorne noted in his pocket diary: "Began to write a Romance" (*CE*, 14:616). The next day he recorded the onset of Una's illness, an illness that he would later write "pierced into [his] very vitals" (*CE*, 14:518) as no previous trouble ever had. Throughout Una's long battle with malaria—or, in the popular name that Hawthorne used, "Roman fever"—Hawthorne drafted *The Marble Faun*, a novel that bears the mark of his feeling of responsibility for his daughter's tortures on the verge of womanhood. This guilt was a complex matter. It was rooted not so much in the fact of his having brought Una to Rome as in the sense of an intimacy abandoned or betrayed. And it was not only his daughter whom Hawthorne sensed he had abandoned, but the part of himself that he associated with her and the literary vocation that gave it expression. Hawthorne's daily struggle to revive his imaginative life by writing *The Marble Faun* and his daily struggle with the prospect that his daughter would never revive coincided exactly. Hawthorne needed to restore his creative self, yet as he worked on his novel he felt more alien from it and more suspicious of it than ever before. He needed, too, to have his daughter restored to him but, on some level, felt that even if she lived their reconciliation was no more possible or desirable than the reconciliation of the opposed elements of his own personality that may be labeled the "patriarchal" and the "daughterly." These ambivalences shape a novel that presents two contrasting models of the daughter-father relationship: in one, the daughter completely subordinates herself to the father and is incorporated into his imperial identity; in the other, she symbolically—or actually—kills her father in a desperate attempt to escape his authority and incestuous domination and to create herself.

In chapter 4 I observed that the criticism of *The Marble Faun* based on the issue of the Fall necessarily assumes that Donatello is the novel's main character. The reading I am presenting here, on the other hand, takes the novel to be more centrally and urgently a story of two women, both defined as artists and as daughters, who are sharply divided and—perhaps in a deeper sense—radically united by the ways in which they fulfill these roles. Hilda identifies herself on three occasions as "a daughter of the Puritans" (54, 362, 466). She is devout, simple, presexual, and unwaveringly submissive to an ideal of patriarchal authority represented for her by the Old Masters. Like Una in Italy, her need for paternal support in a time of uncertainty brings out "Catholic propensities." Hilda's friend Miriam seems to be her inverse. Irreverent, complex, and dangerously sexual, she cannot live—as Hilda does—*through* the figure of the father but only in reaction *against* him. Miriam's origins are unknown, but in each of the speculations about her that the narrator records she has "fled from her paternal home" (23), usually to escape an unsavory father or to avoid sexual domination by a man linked to the father. Like Una in Hawthorne's journals, she betrays a "rich, ill-regulated nature" (280). Miriam is repeatedly described as independent, self-possessed, and even ungovernable, but even before we meet the model these images are qualified by the narrator's remark that "Miriam had great *apparent* freedom of intercourse" (21, my italics). As we discover, Miriam is actually more thoroughly dominated by patriarchal power than is Hilda. The difference between them lies in their responses to the exercise and the agents of this power, and that difference is epitomized in a curious passage from the novel's climactic chapter, "On the Edge of a Precipice."

On a walk among the ruins of the Palace of the Caesars, Kenyon tells his artist friends that they are standing at the site of the legendary chasm that threatened to swallow up classical Rome before the hero Curtius sacrificed himself to save the city. This was the "fatal gulf" into which flowed "all the blood that the Romans shed," Kenyon remarks, including the blood of Virginia, the daughter of a Roman officer, who killed her rather than allow her to be seduced by his commander, the powerful consul Appius Claudius. "Virginia, beyond all question, was stabbed by her father, precisely where we are standing," he concludes. "Then the spot is hallowed forever!" replies Hilda, but Miriam bitterly counters: "Is there such blessed potency in bloodshed?" (163). Hilda views the sacrifice of the daughter to the father's protective authority as sublime—a tragic and noble expression of love on the father's part and the ultimate guarantee against the stains of sexuality and disgrace for the daughter. Miriam, though, seems to find little difference between the seducer and the protector. Both, in the service of their own needs and purposes, violate the daughter, who must fight for her life.

The difference between Hilda's and Miriam's artistic practices may be seen as a function of these antithetical responses to fathers and their claims on daughters. Hilda's is the art of daughterly sacrifice, of the relinquishment of autonomy and even of personal identity in exchange for a spiritual purity and immortality to which the fathers hold the key. The orphan Hilda comes to Rome and is so enthralled by "the mighty Old Masters" (57) that she "cease[s] to consider herself as an original artist" (56). "Reverencing these wonderful men so deeply, she was too grateful for all they bestowed upon her—too loyal—too humble, in their awful presence—to think of enrolling herself in their society. . . . All the youthful hopes and ambitions, the fanciful ideas which she had brought from home . . . were flung aside, and, so far as those most intimate with her could discern, relinquished without a sigh" (57). Hilda's decision to become a copyist, an "exquisitely effective piece of mechanism" for the transmission and reproduction of "the spirit of some great departed Painter" (59), is significantly associated with her gratitude to an artistic patriarchy and her abandonment of the hopes and "fanciful ideas" of youth. These associations oppose her not only to Miriam but also to the storyteller Nathaniel Hawthorne, who indulged in rebellious fancies and pursued, well into the autumn of his life, his youthful ambition to achieve literary distinction.

In contrast to Hilda's exquisite copies, Miriam's compositions are passionate, undisciplined, and strikingly original. Her studio, as we have seen, looks to be perfectly designed to facilitate the unrestricted flight of artistic fancy. Despite these appearances, however, Miriam's imagination is ultimately no less subject to male domination than is Hilda's. Every canvas that Miriam produces contrives to announce its own failure to achieve its desired end. "Over and over again, there was the idea of woman, acting the part of a revengeful mischief towards man," yet these paintings, which begin in celebration, are invariably "given the last touches in utter scorn" (44). The biblical heroines Jael and Judith do not overcome their enemies, even though they slay them, and Miriam's artistic abilities do not win her creative control over her materials: the portraits, she tells Donatello, are "not things that I created but things that haunt me" (45). If Hilda allows herself to be possessed by figures of male power and authority and to become their "instrument" (59), Miriam resists other such figures but

also ends up possessed or haunted by them. The "moral" of her resistance paintings, according to the narrator, is that "woman must strike
through her own heart to reach a human life, whatever were the motives that impelled her" (44). Thus, whether she willingly sacrifices
herself (like Hilda and Virginia) or fights for her life (like Miriam and
Beatrice Cenci), the artist-daughter is destroyed or consumed by the
father.

Beatrice Cenci is closely identified with Miriam throughout *The
Marble Faun*. But she is also the figure through whom Hawthorne
suggests that the situations of Miriam and Hilda may not be as different as they seem. The painted image of Beatrice Cenci, as I noted in
chapter 4, appears more frequently and figures more dramatically in
the novel than does the sculpture of the faun. Indeed, Hawthorne observed in 1848 what a 1909 guidebook to European art subsequently
confirmed: that the painting that hung in the Barberini gallery, identified as a representation of Beatrice by the mannerist Guido Reni, was
"the most generally popular and widely copied portrait in Rome."[10]
Nineteenth-century Americans, in particular, were driven to sentimental raptures by the painting and were plainly titillated by the story that
it recalled. What they responded to in both was a delicious ambiguity.
Beatrice may have been an innocent martyr, raped by a bestial father
and then victimized again by a papal court that falsely accused and
convicted her of complicity in her father's murder. (The court executed
not only Beatrice but her brother and stepmother, leaving no heirs of
the murdered Francesco Cenci and thus entitling the Vatican to claim
his substantial property.) On the other hand, she may have been a
patricide. Moreover, one implicit tenet of domestic ideology was that
a truly pure woman exerted a moral force that protected her from
unwanted sexual advances. Thus, for the nineteenth-century viewers
of her portrait, Beatrice was either the most sanctified and cruelly sacrificed angel of the house or the most alluring and deadly female
Other, or a mixture of both.

Miriam's character, like Beatrice's, is ambiguous, and all the hints
the reader is given about the mysterious "stain" in her past suggest
that her history is to be understood as modeled on the Cenci case. The

fact that her experience is akin to Beatrice's provides a context for Miriam's bitter response when Hilda idealizes the paternal sacrifice of Virginia to prevent her rape: in the Cenci story, the fatherly protector and sexual abuser are the same man. Like the female avengers in her paintings, Miriam, we are led to suppose, has violently resisted or revolted against a powerful figure of male authority, probably a rapacious father. The model is her accomplice in this act of resistance, or she is his. The distribution of responsibility for the act is uncertain, since he seems to have physically committed it. In their private interview, Miriam tells him, "You, at least, have no right to think me [a murderess]," and adds that her hand "had no stain . . . until you grasped it in your own!" (97). But in the same scene she acknowledges that "I am your evil genius, as you mine!" (95). This mutality suggests that they are brother and sister, like Beatrice and Giacomo Cenci. Other evidence tends to support this speculation. The model speaks of knowing Miriam in her girlhood. Later, when she takes a parting look at his corpse (which lies prepared for burial in the Church of the Capuchins because, we discover, at the time of his death the model had been living as a monk, *Brother* Antonio), Miriam sees "the visage that she remembered from a far longer date than the most intimate of her friends suspected" (190). The deed that Miriam and the model commit, "whatever were the motives that impelled" them, consumes both with guilt. But perhaps the greatest horror of Miriam's presumed revolt against a rapacious father is that it neither keeps her from being sexually compromised nor protects her from male domination. On the contrary, the alliance that liberates her from her persecutor only binds her—sexually as well as criminally, Hawthorne implies—to the model, who becomes a new persecutor. And this second unholy relationship leads to a third—her union with Donatello—that frees her from the previous bondage in crime only to take its place.

While Beatrice Cenci's history is linked to Miriam, her image is first associated with Hilda. The figure of Beatrice is introduced in *The Marble Faun* when Hilda shows Miriam the copy of Guido's portrait that she has done from memory, having "[sat] down before the picture, day after day, and let it sink into [her] heart" (65). When Miriam asks whether there was "sin in the deed for which [Beatrice] suffered," Hilda replies, "Her doom is just" (66), whereupon she is "startled to observe that her friend's expression had become almost exactly that of the portrait" (67). Later, though, after she has witnessed the model's murder, Hilda looks in the mirror and finds that her own features have taken on Beatrice's expression. "Am I, too, stained with guilt?" she wonders (205). Hilda has committed no crime, but she nonetheless may be said to resemble the ravished Beatrice in the almost explicitly sexual nature of her relationship to the Old Masters. Asked by Miriam whether Guido might not be jealous that her "Beatrice" so successfully rivals his, Hilda responds in language that equates her creation of a copy with the processes of insemination and childbirth: "Jealous, indeed! . . . If Guido had not wrought through me, my pains would have been thrown away" (68).

One final important instance of the union and division of Hilda and Miriam by the figure of Beatrice Cenci is a painting by a young Italian artist who observes the despondent Hilda in a gallery and grows "deeply interested in her expression" (330). He catches her absorbed in thoughts of Miriam and secretly paints her portrait. When it is displayed, "many connoisseurs" take it to be a variation on Guido's *Beatrice*. The artist entitles his picture *Innocence, dying of a blood-stain,* for it represents Hilda "gazing with sad and earnest horrour, at a blood-spot which she seemed just then to have discovered on her white robe" (330). But his dealer changes the title to *The Signorina's Vengeance*—a label that would have been more appropriate had the model for the painting been Beatrice, or Miriam, rather than Hilda thinking about Miriam. Taken together, these two titles summarize the daughter's options in *The Marble Faun*. Like the sculpted child depicted in the novel's first paragraph, who clasps "a dove to her bosom, but [is] assaulted by a snake," the daughter can choose "Innocence or Evil"—the innocence of devout self-sacrifice or the evil of counterassault. She may die of a bloodstain or take vengeance, but either way she loses her identity, through martyrdom or through transformation (as the Italian's reverent painting is transformed by its change of title) into a terror.

What is the meaning of the stark and destructive daughter-father relations that define, and motivate the actions of, both Miriam and Hilda? My argument has proposed two interrelated answers to this question. One answer is that the choice between victimization and vengeance that confronts these fictional daughters is Hawthorne's projection into the novel of his fear and guilt over Una's grave illness. Una might be sacrificed or, as Sophia and others openly feared, and as Hawthorne's statement that Una's plight had "pierced into [his] very vitals" implies, her ordeal might kill him. At some level of consciousness, I believe, Hawthorne felt that there would be a kind of retributive justice in her bringing about his death. In the novel, he generally treats malaria as a plague brought down upon Rome for the crimes of its history. Sophia, however, made a much more specific connection between the crimes of the Roman fathers and the punishment of Roman fever: "Sovereign Rome [has] slain millions, [and received] for poetically just guerdon the fatal breath of the malaria." Elsewhere, she brought this connection home: "Must Una die because the Roman Emperors outraged the patience of GOD and all human decencies?"[11] These writings show that, in the Hawthorne household, Una's suffering was explicitly linked to patriarchal guilt. But *The Marble Faun* also links Roman fever to filial revolt. The effect of the murder, and then of the encounter with the corpse of Brother Antonio, on Donatello is to make him shake "as with the cold fit of the Roman fever" (196). Thus, Una's illness insinuates itself into Hawthorne's novel both as the curse that the sins of the fathers bring down upon the innocent children and as a symbol and effect of patricidal delirium.

A second way to understand Hawthorne's polarized yet equally doomed fictional daughters is through their relation to Hawthorne himself. Una is identified with aspects of both Miriam and Hilda. But these daughters are also artists, and Hawthorne—whose sense of himself as an artist, as I have shown, involved the acknowledgment of what he considered to be the female element of his personality—identifies with both as well. Hilda's art may be seen as a projection of Hawthorne's hope that he could recover the freshness and inspiration of his own earlier work *and* that he could finally reconcile the two sides of his nature—the imaginative and the practical, the creative and the conservative, the female and the male, the daughterly and the patriarchal. But as Hawthorne labored over *The Marble Faun*, more painstakingly and less confidently and pleasurably than he had worked on any previous novel, I think his hope faded. Like Hilda, he wearied of art. The aesthetic enthusiasms of the early pages are replaced by cynical dismissals not just of individual works but of art in general as the novel increasingly articulates the old practical and moral objections to art that Hawthorne had always associated with father figures. Moreover, the obsessive and ironic repetitions in *The Marble Faun* (which I will discuss further in the next chapter) suggest that Hawthorne perceived himself not as regaining his former creativity but as copying it. Indeed, as Carol Hanberry MacKay has noted, Hawthorne's process of composition in this novel entailed substantial acts of copying of a kind that he had never done before. Hawthorne had reworked and expanded journal entries in composing other tales and romances, but he had not simply reproduced long descriptive passages from his notebooks in any previous work of fiction.[12] Fearing the loss of his own originality, Hawthorne devalues it by approving Hilda's willing sacrifice of hers. But his words of approval do not entirely conceal the note of self-contempt when he remarks that Hilda was right to lay "her individual hopes . . . at the feet" of the Old Masters rather than try to give the world "a picture or two which it would call original; pretty fancies of snow and moonlight; the counterpart, in picture, of so many feminine achievements in literature!" (60–61).

In Miriam, of course, Hawthorne represents the rebellious artist in himself who would defy patriarchal authority rather than submit to it. The 54-year-old father, canonized author, and man of affairs still harbored irreverent and subversive impulses—impulses that had been reawakened, perhaps, by the unsettling stimuli and challenges of his life abroad. But he now found them too threatening. Miriam's vitality, however appealing, must be contained, just as her deed, however justified, must be repudiated. The characterization of Miriam conveys Hawthorne's fear that the price of artistic originality is, symbolically, patricide. In more specific terms, the price is the obliteration of the principle of masculine order and control by the monstrous female Other. The most striking event of the Roman carnival at the end of the novel (in which the revolt against order is the theme) offers an emblem of this sexual and moral subversion. It is Miriam who seems to be the presiding spirit of the carnival as she wanders in and out of the scene disguised as a contadina. Looking for Miriam and Donatello, who have hinted that they will lead him to the lost Hilda, the somber and dignified Kenyon is accosted by "a gigantic female figure, seven feet high, at least, and taking up a third of the street's breadth with the preposterously swelling sphere of her crinoline skirts" (445–46). She singles Kenyon out for affection, and when he will not return it, "the rejected Titaness made a gesture of despair and rage; then suddenly drawing a huge pistol, she took aim right at the obdurate sculptor's breast, and pulled the trigger" (446). This "revengeful damsel" is an image of the guilty Beatrice Cenci, the seductress and murderess, or the guilty Miriam run riot. She may also represent, in Hawthorne's subconscious, a wounded and vengeful Una, punishing her "obdurate" father. And, in some measure, she may be the specter of his own thwarted imaginative life, now threatening to overwhelm him. In any event, she cannot be embraced. Rather, she must be made to relinquish her freedom and power, an act that symbolically takes place later in the same chapter when Miriam is arrested by the Roman authorities and Hilda is released in her stead.

Despite the corruption and violence of most of the father figures in *The Marble Faun*, Hawthorne seems in the end, though with little satisfaction, to cast his lot with them. The novel almost bitterly confirms Kenyon's statement that "the heart of mankind . . . craves a ruler, under whatever title, as a child its father!" To this observation Miriam responds that if there were a "rightful King," she would "lay [her troubles] at his feet" (166). But, in fact, no such king is required to bring both Miriam and Hilda to their knees. Miriam accepts her guilt (for a crime actually committed by Donatello) and a life of penance under a statue of Pope Julius the Third, in whom she sees "the likeness of a father" (316). Though despairing of "so vast a boon," she asks the bronze pontiff's "pardon and paternal affection" (318).

Hilda kneels at the confessional in Saint Peter's and pours out an account of the crime she has witnessed to a priest who promptly reports the matter to the police. And, after being imprisoned briefly in a convent, she goes back to America to be imprisoned for life in Kenyon's heart and home. For both women, the protection of the patriarchy means the abandonment of art.

As for Una, she recovered from Roman fever but in the process underwent a transformation in character that paralleled the exchange of Miriam for Hilda at the end of her father's novel. As Julian Hawthorne later described this change in his sister: "Her intellect was active and capacious, and at one period of her life took a radical turn, questioning and testing all things with a boldness and penetration, combined with a sound impartiality, rare in the feminine mind. But at length the lofty religious bias of her nature triumphed over all doubts" (*Works,* 15:373). The emotional and physical breakdowns that, after her first illness in Rome, plagued Una periodically to the end of her short life may suggest that her lofty religious triumph was not as complete as her brother thought. Nonetheless, she remained a dutiful daughter, sacrificing her chances for an independent life to nurse her aging mother and to compile and copy the fragmentary manuscripts left by her father at his death. Una died and was buried in England, at the age of 33. Her tombstone reads, simply, "Una, Daughter of Nathaniel Hawthorne." Even in death, to paraphrase Hilda, the Old Master would not set her free (334).

7

Fate, Chaos, and Repression

There is a sentence in *The Marble Faun* that sent a shiver down my spine the first time I read it and has done so again each time I have returned to it. I have always found it difficult to say precisely whether my response is a shiver of pleasure or a shiver of discomfort, even horror. But this state of uncertainty and tension, this strange mixture of sensations, is itself an appropriate reaction to the sentence in that it duplicates the sentence's own subject matter and structure.

When we have once known Rome, and left her where she lies, like a long decaying corpse, retaining a trace of the noble shape it was, but with accumulated dust and a fungous growth overspreading all its more admirable features;—left her in utter weariness, no doubt, of her narrow, crooked, intricate streets, so uncomfortably paved with little squares of lava that to tread over them is a penitential pilgrimage, so indescribably ugly, moreover, so cold, so alley-like, into which the sun never falls, and where a chill wind forces its deadly breath into our lungs;—left her, tired of the sight of those immense, seven-storied, yellow-washed hovels, or call them palaces, where all that is dreary in domestic life seems magnified and multiplied, and weary of climbing those staircases, which ascend from a ground-floor of cook-shops, coblers' stalls, stables, and regiments of cavalry, to a middle region of princes, cardinals, and ambassadours, and an upper tier of artists, just beneath the unattainable sky;—left her, worn out with shivering at the cheerless and smoky fireside, by day, and feasting with our own substance the ravenous little populace of a Roman bed, at night;—left her, sick at heart of Italian trickery, which has uprooted whatever faith in man's integrity had endured till now, and sick at stomach of sour bread, sour wine, rancid butter, and bad cookery, needlessly bestowed on evil meats;—left her, disgusted with the pretense of Holiness and the reality of Nastiness, each equally omnipresent;—left her, half-lifeless from the languid atmosphere, the vital principle of which has been used up, long ago, or corrupted by myriads of slaughters;—left her, crushed down in spirit with the desolation of her ruin, and the hopelessness of her future;—left her, in short, hating her with all our might, and adding our individual curse to the Infinite Anathema which her old crimes have unmistakeably brought down;—when we have left Rome in such mood as this, we are astonished by the discovery, by-and-by, that our heart-strings have mysteriously attached themselves to the Eternal City, and are drawing us thitherward again, as if it were more familiar, more intimately our home, than even the spot where we were born! (325–26).

Rhetorically, this sentence achieves its effect through the tension between what we might call its energy of expansion and its energy of contraction, or its centrifugal and its centripetal force. As the movement away from the center—Rome—is repeated and insisted upon with greater and greater vehemence ("left her . . .; left her . . .; left her"), one becomes increasingly aware of Rome's abiding presence. With each new assertion of Rome's abandonment, Rome returns and seems all the more inescapable. There is a thrill ("we are astonished") in the sentence's suggestion of an underlying order, a still point that is unaffected by all these departures and verbal wanderings, a sense of destiny or fatality. There is a thrill, too, in its suggestion of the radical instability of our identities, of the uninterpretability of our desires, of our literal incapacity to know for sure whether we are coming or going. These opposing thrills, attended by mingled feelings of awe and fear, are the components of the experience of the uncanny, as Freud defines it.

In chapter 5 I mentioned Freud's essay on the uncanny in connection with the tendency of the "homelike" and the "unhomelike" to merge or change places in *The Marble Faun*. The sentence cited above, in which a thoroughly alien Rome reveals itself to be "more familiar, more our home, than even the spot where we were born," is another instance of the ambivalence or instability of "home" in the novel. We might notice, too, the relevance of this sentence—in which Rome is personified as a monstrous female body that revolts yet "mysteriously" attracts "us"—to the theme of the female Other that we took up in chapter 6. In this chapter, though, the sentence will help us to pose and explore some of the existential questions of Hawthorne's novel—questions about the nature of human identity and the conditions of human knowledge. Is the course of a human life determined, fated, cast from the start in an unbreakable mold, or, at the other extreme, is it a series of random, chaotic, incoherent events? Are there meanings in human experience that a mind probing deeply enough may discover, or is meaning what the mind produces by selective resistance to experience, by repressing everything that it cannot or does not wish to understand?

The philosophical ideas of fate and chaos, and the psychological mechanism of repression, are important features of the long sentence that marks Kenyon's and the novel's return to Rome after a 110-page escape into the country. Fate, chaos, and repression also figure significantly in Freud's definition of the uncanny. These are the concepts that we will use to effect our final critical transformation of *The Marble Faun*. At first, such concepts and the questions to which they pertain may seem abstract. But by the end of the chapter they will have led us back to some quite material and immediate social and political dimensions of the novel we might not otherwise have seen.

Freud defines the uncanny as "that class of the frightening which leads back to what is known of old and long familiar," or, more specifically, as the "instances of frightening things . . . in which the frightening element can be shown to be something repressed which *recurs*"

(Freud, 220, 241). One personal illustration of the uncanny that Freud offers is especially pertinent to *The Marble Faun* and to the passage about the attraction of Rome that we have been considering:

> As I was walking, one hot summer afternoon, through the deserted streets of a provincial town in Italy which was unknown to me, I found myself in a quarter of whose character I could not long remain in doubt. Nothing but painted women were to be seen at the windows of the small houses, and I hastened to leave the narrow street at the next turning. But after having wandered about for a time without enquiring my way, I suddenly found myself back in the same street, where my presence was now beginning to excite attention. I hurried away once more, only to arrive by another *detour* at the same place yet a third time. Now, however, a feeling overcame me which I can only describe as uncanny. (Freud, 237)

Freud's anecdote, like Hawthorne's sentence, is a dramatic enactment of the return of the repressed. The particular desire that Freud repressed—the illicit desire for foreign and "painted" women—also links his story to *The Marble Faun,* in which the woman painter Miriam, a feminized Rome, and the Catholic Church (referred to in the anti-Catholic speeches and writings of Hawthorne's time as "the whore of Babylon") are all illicit objects of desire. Beyond their structural and thematic similarities, Freud's and Hawthorne's narratives both convey a feeling that may be described as a strange combination of the sense of fatality and the sense of chaos. This is the experience of the uncanny. From one standpoint, Freud's unavoidable return to the street of the prostitutes, or Hawthorne's to Rome, indicates a determined universe, one in which all our steps are plotted and our lives fated. From another, as Freud's sense of being lost or Hawthorne's astonishment implies, these same events indicate that we experience the universe as chaotic, a labyrinthine place in which results do not follow from intentions and in which, from moment to moment, we do not know where or even who we are.

In literature, Freud observes, the effect of the uncanny is most often produced in the following ways: when an inanimate object is transformed into an animate one, and vice versa; when an uncertainty is produced as to whether a figure is a human being or something else; when the device of the "double" is used; when the primitive sense of an animistic universe is evoked, particularly a universe in which the spirits of the dead have power over the living; and, finally, "when the distinction between imagination and reality is effaced" (Freud, 244). This catalog of the ways in which literature represents the uncanny might be taken for a summary of Hawthorne's techniques in *The Marble Faun*. Each device that Freud mentions is present in the novel, and each is used in connection with the one character whom we have not yet closely examined: Miriam's model.

The model is introduced in a chapter entitled "Subterranean Reminiscences," in which Miriam encounters him among the corpses in the Catacomb of Saint Calixtus. In the next chapter, "The Spectre of the Catacomb," he follows Miriam back into the light and, metaphorically, into life. Thus, the model's very emergence from the depths of the earth and from Miriam's denied memories and fled past is represented as a return of the repressed. From the beginning, too, the model is associated with the dead hand of the Roman past that continues to exert a stranglehold upon the present. His appearance recalls the legend of Memmius, the "Man-Demon" who was condemned to wander forever in the catacombs for his rejection of Christianity but could win brief holidays above ground by prevailing on unwary visitors "to take him by the hand, and guide him out into the daylight." During these periods, Memmius "would gratify his fiendish malignity by perpetrating signal mischief on his benefactor, and perhaps bringing some old pestilence or other forgotten and long-buried evil on society—or, possibly, teaching the modern world some decayed and dusty kind of crime, which the antique Romans knew—and then would hasten back to the catacomb" (33). Accordingly, the model comes back to haunt Miriam, affecting her much as Hawthorne claims that Rome affects its visitors: by pressing down or crowding out the present moment under the weight and density of "ponderous remembrances" and "a by-gone life."

The model seems an embodiment of fate itself, yet at the same time he is a figure without a single, fixed identity who may be seen to stand for the instability, or even the fictionality, of human character.

This is the significance of his occupation as an artist's model. "He looked as if he might just have stept out of a picture, and, in truth, was likely enough to find his way into a dozen pictures; being no other than one of those living models, dark, bushy bearded, wild of aspect and attire, whom artists convert into Saints or assassins, according as their pictorial purposes demand" (19). In this first description of the model, Hawthorne plays with the idea of his multiple roles and of their range of moral values ("Saints or assassins"). The fact that these divergent values are assigned to him by artists for "their pictorial purposes," and that he has no necessary relation to them, underscores the uncertainty of his own identity. As described here, he is the figure in whom, to use Freud's phrase, "the distinction between imagination and reality is effaced." Stepping in and out of pictures, he is an actual being who is a model for imaginary beings and who looks as if he might himself be the work of an artist's imagination come to life.

As the narrative progresses, the model seems in fact to step in and out of works of art and in and out of mortal life. On the night of the murder, Hilda, Miriam, Kenyon, and Donatello discover a portfolio of old drawings among which Hilda recognizes a preliminary sketch for Guido's painting of the Archangel Michael setting his foot upon a demon. The demon's face, everyone but Miriam exclaims, is identical to that of Miriam's model. Agreeing to meet the next day at the Church of the Capuchins to examine the demon's face in the finished painting, the company takes the midnight ramble that ends on the Tarpeian Rock. There, the model emerges from "a deep, empty niche [in the wall of the palace built on the rock], that had probably once contained a statue" (171), is flung over the edge by Donatello, and lands "stone dead" (173). The following morning, when all the friends except Hilda arrive at the Church of the Capuchins to see Guido's painted demon, they find the actual body of the model displayed for burial as the monk Brother Antonio. He is scheduled to be buried in another "niche" (194), this time a niche in the crypt beneath the church, but even death does not end his transfigurations. The burial plots beneath the church are limited, Miriam is told, and monks rest in them for only 30 years before their skeletons are dug up to accommodate others.

Miriam's model, then, is associated with metamorphoses between the human and the nonhuman. He is a figure from the realm of the dead who haunts the living, and a figure of imagination who seems to step into actual existence and out again. But perhaps his most uncanny role is that of a double for Donatello, who would seem to be his opposite. Donatello is depicted as a representative of youth, innocence, immediacy, and the country; the model represents age, guilt, memory, and the city. Yet their characters converge in the novel. Donatello himself, of course, is introduced as a figure of imagination who has stepped into actual life, and as a nonhuman or incompletely human creature in the process of transformation into a man. He is the faun. The model, when he first emerges from the gloom of the catacombs, appears to be something quite similar. "He was clad in a voluminous cloak, that seemed to be made of a buffalo's hide, and a pair of those goat-skin breeches, with their hair outward, which are still commonly worn by the peasants of the Roman Campagna. In this garb, they look like antique Satyrs; and, in truth, the Spectre of the Catacomb might have represented the last survivor of that vanished race, hiding himself in sepulchral gloom, and mourning over his lost life of woods and streams" (30). Later, after he has killed the model and assumed his place in the bond of guilt with Miriam, Donatello—the last survivor of the race of Monte Beni—does hide himself in sepulchral gloom and mourn over his lost life of woods and streams. Miriam's model, it appears, is also the model for Donatello, a relationship that is reinforced by the legend that the Monte Beni line originated when a satyr "loved a mortal maiden, and (perhaps by kindness, and the subtle courtesies which love might teach to his simplicity, or possibly by a ruder wooing) . . . won her to his haunts" (233). Miriam herself suggests this relationship well before the murder when, frolicking with Donatello in the Borghese Gardens, she demands that he "make [her] known to [his] kindred," and adds: "Do not fear that I shall shrink, even if one of your rough cousins, a hairy Satyr, should come capering on his goat-legs out of the haunts of far antiquity, and propose to dance with me among these lawns!" (78). Before the end of this scene, the model has done precisely that.

Satyrs are customarily associated with sexual appetite and aggression, fauns with innocence. But, in fact, they are two names for the same thing. A satyr is a Greek sylvan deity, usually conceived as part man, part goat; a faun is the Roman name for such a creature. Significantly, the marble statue of a faun that Hawthorne saw in Rome and appropriated for his novel's central image was identified, in the tourist's guidebook that Hawthorne used, not as the work of the Greek sculptor Praxiteles but as a Roman copy. It was also titled *Resting Satyr*. Thus, the model for Hawthorne's marble faun as well as for his living faun, Donatello, is a satyr. In both cases, the artist has disguised or changed a figure's character by giving it a different name.

The identity of Hawthorne's novel, then, arises out of an initial verbal transformation of a resting satyr into a marble faun. In this respect, *The Marble Faun* is like the young Italian artist's painting of Hilda, the original title of which—*Innocence, dying of a blood-stain*—is changed to *The Signorina's Vengeance*. In each work, difference is created by language. The same image—a woodland creature or a young woman staring at a bloodstain on her white dress—takes on an entirely different meaning depending on what it is called. The painted image of a violated sexual and moral innocent becomes one of a violent murderess when its title is changed. The sculpted image of a resting satyr that is renamed a marble faun undergoes the same transformation but in the opposite direction: the satyr's aggressive sexuality and dark experience is replaced by the childlike innocence of the faun. These examples, along with the question of Beatrice Cenci's character discussed in chapter 6 and the question of the Fortunate Fall discussed in chapter 4, suggest that the world of *The Marble Faun* is one in which meaning is unstable and indeterminate, or is determined only by arbitrary manipulations of words. It is, we might say, the world of the model.

Miriam's model, as we have seen, incarnates this principle of instability by his multiple transformations of identity. His occupation, too, in which he makes himself available for pictorial conversion into saints or assassins, exemplifies meaning's arbitrary and artificial production. It is significant that Hilda becomes disillusioned with the religious art that once uplifted her when she loses her capacity to ignore the fact that the Old Masters' divine subjects were painted from human models. Their Holy Virgins, for instance, may often have been modeled on their mistresses. Through a religious title or manipulations of Christian iconography, Hilda perceives, painters might pass off celebrations of their lusts as expressions of spiritual love. This dark suspicion causes art to lost its "consecration" for Hilda (341); once admired works now convey only "an inevitable hollowness" and appear to her as "crust[s] of paint over an emptiness" (338, 341). As these descriptions suggest, Hilda's initiation into the world of the model disillusions her not only with art but, to some degree, with life as well. The meaning and order that had inhered in experience, as consecration had inhered for her in the art of the Old Masters, begin to seem artificially and superficially applied, painted over an emptiness. For the first time in her life abroad, Hawthorne writes, Hilda's self-possession is shaken and she yearns for the "native homeliness" of her American village (342). One mark of Hilda's entanglement in the world of the model during this period, and of its threat to her personal identity, is, of course, the young Italian's painting, in which she herself serves as the unwitting model for an image that is generally taken to be a likeness of Beatrice Cenci.

The images of Beatrice and the model are endlessly copied in works of art. But, more ominously, they seem to stamp themselves again and again on the experience of Hawthorne's characters as though modern life were what Miriam accuses modern sculpture of being: a series of figures and attitudes copied from a handful of antique prototypes (124). These models seem fatal, determinative, yet at the same time, as we have seen, they are associated with instability, uncertainty, chaos. How are we to explain this ambivalent—or uncanny—character of the world of the model? A formal explanation is suggested by our treatment of competing artistic values and media in chapter 5. *The Marble Faun* is, in some measure, a novel about the theory and practice of art, and art is always produced out of the tension between fixity and change, the encounter between what T. S. Eliot famously called "tradition" and "the individual talent." There is also a social and historical explanation, though, for the novel's seemingly

contradictory representation of identity as at once determined and unstable. In the middle of the nineteenth century, economic, technologi-
cal, and demographic changes in America were creating a society in
which many individuals felt simultaneously more interdependent with,
even undifferentiated from, others and more isolated and unanchored
than ever before.

The increased division and mechanization of labor necessary for
factory production, the growing concentration of people in cities, and
the early development of instruments of mass culture helped generate
the sense of dependency and the impulse to conformity against which
Emerson railed in the 1830s and 1840s when he insisted that "society
everywhere is in conspiracy against the manhood of every one of its
members" and pronounced that "imitation is suicide" (Emerson, 261,
259). Meanwhile, the ethos of competitive individualism was becoming more deeply entrenched—an ethos reinforced by the breakdown
of the family's role in economic production, by the often forced mo-
bility of the population, and by the mysterious cycles of boom and
bust that individuals could not control but had to struggle (often
against one another) to survive. Competitive individualism brought
with it an increased sense of the self's isolation and uncertainty. Thus,
the same Ralph Waldo Emerson who excoriated the conformity he
saw all around him also lamented that each individual is locked in the
perspectival and temperamental prison of his own identity, cut off
from others and from any possibility of apprehending an uncolored,
undistorted truth.

In its wanderings and its returns, its vacillations between resistance to definition and closure and insistence upon them, *The Marble
Faun* seeks to escape both the determinacy and the indeterminacy of
meaning, the fatality and the chaos of life. After the model's murder,
a deed that is described as taking only an instant "to grave itself in the
eternal adamant" (171), Donatello is sunk in guilt and flees from Miriam, Hilda recoils from all three of her friends, and the novel seems to
have arrived at a dead end, a bleak moral standstill. The only way to
go on, for the characters and the author, is to wander. To wander is
to resist the finality and fatality of "the eternal adamant," as Haw-

thorne implies when he begins the chapter that projects the novel's action into the countryside by stating that "we must now . . . endeavor to make our story flow onward, like a streamlet" (213). The fluidity of the stream holds out the possibility that the course and meaning of *The Marble Faun* are not cast in stone. (In fact, this tension between water and stone is reproduced several times in images of marble fountains that are designed, of course, to contain water and to force its flow to assume certain patterns, but that have themselves been eroded and redesigned by the water's circulation.)

A sense of the same possibility animates Kenyon's plan to free Donatello from his self-entombment in the tower of Monte Beni by persuading him to "ramble among these hills and valleys." "The little adventures and vicissitudes of travel will do him infinite good," Kenyon tells Miriam. "After his recent profound experience, he will recreate the world by the new eyes with which he will regard it" (284). For a while, the plan works. The rambling Tuscan towns, which display much ingenious reclamation of ancient rubble, seem to bear out the idea that growth and new life may emerge out of ruin and decay. The past is so completely overcome that, for the only time in the novel, Hawthorne lapses into the present tense in his account of his characters' movements: Kenyon "draws bridle" at a winery and "calls for a goblet," Donatello "alights where a shrine, with a burning lamp before it, is built into the wall of an inn-stable," and at last "our two travellers resume their way" across "the broad valley with a mist so thinly scattered over it as to be perceptible only in the distance" (294–95). The next paragraph, though, dispels the mist, the tense, and the idea that the world can be recreated by perceiving it anew. "Immediately about them, however, there were abundant tokens that the country was not really the paradise it looked to be, at a casual glance" (295). Ultimately, the casual ramble leads not to renewal but to illusion. Therefore, Hawthorne and Donatello end up "converting the otherwise aimless journey into a penitential pilgrimage" (296) that leads to the base of the bronze pontiff in Perugia and, finally, back to Rome.

Hawthorne begins the last chapter of *The Marble Faun* with a plea that his reader allow him the imaginative latitude that romance requires. "The Gentle Reader, we trust, would not thank us for one of those minute elucidations, which are so tedious, and, after all, so unsatisfactory, in clearing up the romantic mysteries of a story" (455). His work is a multicolored tapestry that is "more easily rent than mended," and he entreats the reader to "accept it at its worth, without tearing the web apart, with the idle purpose of discovering how its threads have been knit together." Besides, he observes, "the actual experience of even the most ordinary life is full of events that never explain themselves, either as regards their origin or their tendency" (455). Here, again, Hawthorne's impulse to resist fixity or closure is in evidence. The chromatic image (reminiscent of the stained-glass windows that Kenyon takes to be symbols of Catholicism's mystifications) should not be destroyed in pursuit of some white light of discovery, nor should human life be seen as a series of events drawn from preestablished models that explain experience's origin and set its course.

To lack a known origin and a defined tendency, however, is to be a homeless wanderer. *The Marble Faun* obviously conveyed something of this experience of instability to its early readers, who demanded explanations that Hawthorne quickly composed the postscript to provide. There, he concludes that his readers' insistence on examining "the wrong side of the tapestry" (455), as he had called it, proves his book to have been "a failure" (464). Yet, he adds, speaking of "the Author" in the third person: "To confess the truth, he was himself troubled with a curiosity similar to that which he has just deprecated on the part of his readers" (464). It is significant that, in this postscript, the narrator explicitly joins "his friends, Hilda and the sculptor" (464), in their intention to return to America to take up "the reality of life" (461). Earlier in the novel he had criticized "the iron rule in our days, to require an object and a purpose in life," adding: "No life now wanders like an unfettered stream; there is a mill-wheel for the tiniest rivulet to turn. We go all wrong, by too strenuous a resolution to go all right" (239). But in the end the narrator endorses and shares Hilda's and Kenyon's purpose of quitting their foreign wanderings, which, if allowed to go on too long, threaten to efface completely the distinction between the "homelike" and the "unhomelike" (and, implicitly, between right and wrong). "We defer the reality of life, in such cases, until a future moment, when we shall again breathe our native air; but, by-and-by, there are no future moments; or, if we do return, we find that the native air has lost its invigorating quality, and that life has shifted its reality to the spot where we have deemed ourselves only temporary residents. . . . It is wise, therefore, to come back betimes—or never" (461).

The Marble Faun never actually takes its Americans home. In fact, America, as it exists in Hawthorne's novel, is a symbolic construct, a foil to the foreignness or "otherness" of Italy, not a real place. Although it is repeatedly identified with "actualities" (3) and with "the reality of life," the America that appears in the novel bears little resemblance to the country to which Hawthorne returned in 1860. The letters Hawthorne wrote from Rome show him to have been aware of the actualities that most concerned American society and challenged the status of the United States as a nation in the late 1850s. In *The Marble Faun*, however, these actualities are not so much escaped as they are repressed.

The role of repression in generating the novel, and particularly in establishing the tension between America and Italy that gives it shape, is apparent in Hawthorne's preface. "No author, without a trial, can conceive of the difficulty of writing a Romance about a country where there is no shadow, no antiquity, no mystery, no picturesque and gloomy wrong, nor anything but a common-place prosperity, in broad and simple daylight, as is happily the case with my dear native land. It will be very long, I trust, before romance-writers may find congenial and easily handled themes either in the annals of our stalwart Republic, or in any characteristic and probable events of our individual lives" (3). Here, Hawthorne represses the memory of his own American romances, which have already done what he claims to "trust" romance writers will not be able to do for a long time. What is *The Scarlet Letter* if not a romance that draws its materials and themes from "the annals of our stalwart Republic"? What is *The Blithedale Romance* if not a work based on the characteristic—and not only probable but actual—events in the lives of American social reformers of the 1840s, events that were part of Hawthorne's own life? The passage quoted above almost seems to elicit thoughts of these novels as it implicitly denies their existence. The repressed, as Freud argued, returns. And it returns even more pointedly and hauntingly in Hawthorne's characterization of America as a unified and uniform society, without "shadow" or "gloomy wrong" or "anything but a common-place prosperity, in broad and simple daylight." America is defined by these images as the state of freedom from two scourges: division and darkness. But these same images inevitably call forth the "shadow" and "gloomy wrong" that, as everyone in 1859 knew, had bitterly divided America and threatened to destroy it: the shadow of black slavery. I am not about to argue that *The Marble Faun* is at bottom an allegory of American race relations. I do want to propose, though, that the issue of race is a repressed element of the novel, one that is unsettlingly linked for Hawthorne both to the force of fate and to the prospect of chaos, and that its returns constitute the novel's most uncanny effects.

It is only a slight exaggeration to say that Hawthorne's residence in Rome was itself made possible by his literary handling of the slavery question years before. His lucrative appointment as U.S. consul in England in 1853, and the opportunity for European travel that it afforded after his term, was the reward for writing the campaign biography of his friend Franklin Pierce, who was elected president in 1852. Pierce, a New Hampshire Democrat, faced strong opposition in the North for his unwillingness to oppose southern slavery and for his support of the Compromise of 1850, which instituted the Fugitive Slave Law and allowed for the expansion of slavery into some western territories. In his biography Hawthorne defends Pierce's position, emphasizing the candidate's love for his "whole, united, native country," which Hawthorne describes as a "great and sacred reality" that "Providence had brought into [being]" (*Works*, 12:371, 415). The forcible abolition of slavery, he continues, might result in "the aggravated injury of those whose condition it aimed to ameliorate" and in "the ruin of two races" (*Works*, 12:415).

Here, Hawthorne manages to hold in tension the seemingly incompatible ideas of a sacred, united America and an America com-

prised of two unequal races and divided by the evil of slavery into two
hostile regions. As hostilities continued to escalate later in the decade,
though, Hawthorne himself could not sustain either the image of
America or the position on abolition that he presented in his *Life of
Franklin Pierce*. His statements about the abolitionist cause are inconsistent. Late in 1855 he wrote to Ticknor from Liverpool: "If anything
could bring me back to America, this winter, it would undoubtedly be
my zeal for the Anti-slavery cause; but my official engagements render
it quite impossible to assist personally" (*CE*, 17:414). Almost two
years later, though, he responded with annoyance at the receipt of an
abolitionist pamphlet written by Sophia's sister, the social activist Elizabeth Peabody. Drawing on his consular experience, he made an argument that echoed his claim in the Pierce biography that abolition
would worsen the condition of those it meant to help and convicted
his sister-in-law of naïveté: "Now, I presume you think the abolition
of flogging was a vast boon to seamen. I see, on the contrary, with
perfect distinctness, that many murders and an immense mass of un-
punishable cruelty—a thousand blows, at least, for every one that the
cat-of-nine-tails would have inflicted—have resulted from that very
thing. There is a moral in this fact which I leave you to deduce" (*CE*,
18:116). However he may have vacillated on the question of what to
do about slavery, Hawthorne's letters from Europe clearly chart his
gradual abandonment of the notion of America as a "whole, united"
country, a "great and sacred" work of Providence. Writing to Horatio
Bridge early in 1857, he remarked that "the States are too various and
extended to form really one country" and suggested that he had long
thought so (*CE*, 18:8). Shortly before his return three years later, he
wrote to Ticknor: "I go for a dissolution of the Union; and on that
ground, I hope the Abolitionists will push matters to extremity" (*CE*,
18:227). By late 1860 he had come to believe that "the Union [was]
unnatural, a scheme of man, not an ordinance of God" (*CE*, 18:355).

The issues of slavery and of the nature and future of the American
union are nowhere addressed in *The Marble Faun*, yet the novel bears
some indications of their presence in Hawthorne's consciousness. To
begin with, it is a book filled with master-slave relationships. Indeed,
Kenyon's first "true glimpse" of Miriam's situation is when he sees her

as a slave, kneeling to her master, the model, in a Roman piazza: "What a terrible thraldom did it suggest! Free as she seemed to be— beggar as he looked—the nameless vagrant must then be dragging the beautiful Miriam through the streets of Rome, fettered and shackled more cruelly than any captive queen of yore" (108). American slavery more directly intrudes on Hawthorne's narrative in the scene at the Trevi Fountain on the night of the model's murder. Observing the gushing, swirling fountain, one of the group of touring artists suggests that, in America, this water might "turn the machinery of a cotton-mill," and another remarks that it might also be used in "cleansing the national flag of any stains that it may have incurred" (146). The reference to processing cotton, the principal crop of the slave economy, leaves no doubt as to the nature of the stain on the American flag.

The problem of the sacredness or profanity of the Union—the question of whether it can claim divine sanction—that we have seen Hawthorne debate in his letters and in the Pierce biography also arises, curiously transformed, in *The Marble Faun*. The terms used to evaluate the union of Miriam and Donatello on market day in Perugia are the same ones with which Hawthorne characterizes the United States in the cited passages from those other writings. "The bond betwixt you," Kenyon tells his friends, "is a true one, and never—except by Heaven's own act—should be rent asunder" (321). Providence "recognizes your union," he continues, so long as it is understood that "your bond is twined with . . . black threads" (322). Providentially joined, yet also, in Miriam's words, "miserably entangled . . . by a bond of guilt" (322), the couple stands in a paradoxical relationship similar to the one that Hawthorne perceived to exist between the northern and southern states, and between black and white Americans, in the 1850s. Still, we might reasonably wonder whether this similarity is not a meaningless coincidence. After all, guilty sexual unions are common and long-standing elements in Hawthorne's fiction. And the prominence of images of whiteness and blackness in *The Marble Faun* need not imply the influence of the American political scene on his imagination. These are images that typically convey abstract states of goodness and evil, or innocence and guilt, in Hawthorne's work, as they do in the rhetoric of Puritanism in which he was steeped. Yet Miriam and Donatello, unlike previous characters in Hawthorne's fiction, are linked to the slavery question and the question of America's future in one striking way: in their individual persons and in their union, they embody the problem of racial difference and of racial mixture.

Donatello and Miriam are mysterious and morally ambiguous figures in *The Marble Faun*. And their mystery and ambiguity, the novel suggests, are matters of racial identity. Hawthorne uses the word *race*—which, in the nineteenth century, often loosely designated nationality or ethnicity—in connection with both characters. Donatello is repeatedly depicted as the latest representative of "the race of Monte Beni" (231), and the question that is raised throughout has to do with the relationship between this race and fully human beings. As described, the race of modern fauns is at once a pure race—innocent of human sinfulness—and already a mixed race. Having originated, according to legend, in the union of a satyr and a woman, it is said to combine "the characteristics of the brute creation . . . with those of humanity" (9). Miriam is human, but, like the faun, her origins are mysterious and subject to imaginative speculation. From the start, moreover, that speculation characterizes her, too, in terms of racial difference and racial mixture. There is "a certain rich Oriental character in her face," and many take her to be Jewish (22). Or, interestingly, she is thought to be "the offspring of a Southern American planter, who had given her an elaborate education and endowed her with his wealth; but the one burning drop of African blood in her veins so affected her with a sense of ignominy, that she relinquished all, and fled her country" (23). Even at the end, when Miriam is identified as neither a Jew nor a mulatto but the daughter of an English mother and an Italian father, Hawthorne still imagines and refers to her as a woman of "mixed race" (430).

These characterizations exemplify the general and pervasive presence of the theme of race in *The Marble Faun*. The figure of the faun, however, may link this theme more specifically and insistently to the crucial American issue of the period, the place of blacks in the Union and in white society. The most extended of the few references to blacks in Hawthorne's early notebooks concerns "a genuine specimen of the slave-negro" whom Hawthorne encountered in western Massachusetts and described as "a queer thing of mere feeling, with some glimmerings of sense" (*CE*, 8:112). The image might well be that of the faun, "an amiable and sensual creature, easy, mirthful, apt for jollity, yet not incapable of being touched by pathos," or even of being "educated through the medium of his emotions; so that the coarser, animal portion of his nature might eventually be thrown into the background, though never utterly expelled" (9). In fact, the question that Hawthorne raises in the Pierce biography, as to whether the eradication of slavery—and of the absolute distinction between black and white that it signified—might result in "the ruin of two races," is the novel's question about the effect of the mixture of innocent animal instinct and human self-consciousness in the faun. This connection is confirmed, I think, by an extraordinary passage from the 1862 essay, "Chiefly about War Matters," in which Hawthorne presents "one very pregnant token of a social system thoroughly disturbed" (*Works*, 12:318).

This "token" is a party of escaped slaves fleeing through rural Virginia toward Washington, D.C. Hawthorne writes:

> So rudely were they attired,—as if their garb had grown upon them spontaneously,—and so picturesquely natural in their manners, and wearing such a crust of primeval simplicity (which is quite polished away from the northern black man), that they seemed a kind of creature by themselves, not altogether human, but perhaps quite as good, and *akin to the fauns and rustic deities of olden times*. . . . For the sake of the manhood which is latent in them, I would not have turned them back; but I should have felt almost as reluctant, on their own account, to hasten them forward to the stranger's land. (*Works*, 12:318–19, my italics)

As Hawthorne views them, these unsophisticated rural black men about to enter the capital city are fauns, Donatellos, on the verge of a transformation that, the passage suggests, promises to be both a rise and a fall. Up until this point in the passage, though, the escaping slaves are seen as strangers, "a kind of creature by themselves." They are observed dispassionately, from a distance; whatever their origin and their fate may be, they do not implicate Hawthorne and his readers. But the very next paragraph obliterates this comfortable distance between black and white Americans as it extends the reference of "a social system thoroughly disturbed" to include not just the war-torn South of 1862 but the United States from its inception.

"There is an historical circumstance, known to few, that connects the children of the Puritans with these Africans of Virginia in a very singular way. They are our brethren, as being lineal descendants from the Mayflower, the fated womb of which, in her first voyage, sent forth a brood of Pilgrims on Plymouth Rock, and, in a subsequent one, spawned slaves upon the Southern soil,—a monstrous birth, but with which we have an instinctive sense of kindred, and so are stirred by an irresistible impulse to attempt their rescue, even at the cost of blood and ruin. The character of our sacred ship, I fear, may suffer a little by this revelation; but we must let her white progeny offset her dark one,—and two such portents never sprang from an identical source before" (*Works*, 12:319). The effect of this image of the Mayflower as the womb from which sprang both "the children of the Puritans" and "these Africans of Virginia" may be described as uncanny. Literally, it reveals the unhomelike to be homelike, the black Other to be a brother and a double. What this revelation implies, moreover, is that the convergence of former slaves on Washington, D.C., the political center and symbol of American identity, is not to be understood as a flight "to the stranger's land" but as the return of the repressed. America was never, as *The Marble Faun* sometimes conceives it to be, a place of "pure white light"; therefore, the debates and finally the war over slavery could never represent—as many believed they did— the nation's fortunate or unfortunate fall from innocence. From its sacred origins, Hawthorne's story of the Mayflower suggests, America had been monstrously mixed.

Slavery was the most important of a number of issues that divided mid-nineteenth-century Americans and challenged some of the idealized popular images of the nation and its origins. During the last years of his residence abroad, Hawthorne, as we have seen, often expressed his own feelings of disillusionment with America. His country increasingly seemed to him to lack a principle of organic unity that might help it through what he called the "miserable confusion" (*CE*, 18:227) of its current political crisis. Hawthorne's disillusionment offers one context within which we may understand the intense concern of his late works with lost purity and with recovering origins. *The Marble Faun* exemplifies this concern in its interest in Donatello and "The Pedigree of Monte Beni" (231) and in its celebration of Hilda's efforts to retrieve old masterpieces of art, to capture originals—even those "darkened into an indistinct shadow, through time and neglect, or . . . injured by cleaning, or retouched by some profane hand"—in their "pristine glory" (59).

Other writings of Hawthorne's final years, however, seek to recover glory, clarity, and order not in ancient legend or in the art of the Italian Renaissance but in England, America's fatherland, and in the cultural legacy that it still may hold for "the children of the Puritans." His last published book is a collection of essays about England, significantly entitled *Our Old Home*. And the unfinished novel manuscripts that he left at his death revolve around the attempts of an American to reclaim his family property and reenter his family history in England. Years before he was given the opportunity to live in England, Hawthorne had described, in the sketch "Fragments from the Journal of a Solitary Man," the appeal of regaining a connection with his ancestral home: "And England, the land of my ancestors! Once I fancied that my sleep would not be quiet in the grave unless I should return, as it were, to my home of past ages, and see the very cities, and castles, and battle-fields of history, and stand within the holy gloom of its cathedrals, and kneel at the shrines of its immortal poets, there asserting myself their hereditary countryman" (*CE*, 11:315). Going back beyond the Mayflower to America's prehistory in England, however, did not afford Hawthorne a vision of his Anglo-Saxon heritage in its "pristine glory." In fact, his feelings about the "old home" he came to know were decidedly mixed. Ironically, too, at the center of the society of his ancestors, in the mansion of the lord mayor of London, he found installed the representatives of a "race" quite foreign to him and far more ancient than his own—a people who, in the Western imagination, epitomized racial otherness as much as did blacks from Africa.

David Salomons, the lord mayor of London who honored U.S. Consul Hawthorne with a banquet at the Mansion House in April 1856, was a Jew. Salomons's religion had made his political career a difficult one, but with the help of a prominent and well-connected family he overcame the stigma of his Jewishness and such early humiliations as having been removed from his seat in the House of Commons when, in the oath of office, he substituted the words "so help me God" for "on the true faith of a Christian." Several months before he entertained Hawthorne, Salomons had been praised by the *Illustrated London Times* as one of "those modern 'merchant princes' who emulate the House of Medici, in their patronage of art and its votaries."[1] And, in a curious way, Salomons would serve as Hawthorne's patron—or at least as a provider of materials for his art—as well. For at his dinner Hawthorne was seated across from the woman who became the model for Miriam in his Italian romance and the man whose image he recalled in creating Miriam's tormenter.

The passage in Hawthorne's *English Notebooks* that describes his response to Emma Abigail Salomons, the lord mayor's sister-in-law, is one of the most remarkable and revealing in his work.

My eyes were mostly drawn to a young lady who sat nearly opposite me, across the table. She was, I suppose, dark, and yet not dark, but rather seemed to be of pure white marble, yet not white; but the purest and finest complexion, (without a shade of color in it, yet anything but sallow or sickly) that I ever beheld. Her hair was a wonderful deep, raven black, black as night, black as death; *not* raven black, for that has a shiny gloss, and her's [*sic*] had not; but it was hair never to be painted, nor described—wonderful hair, Jewish hair. Her nose had a beautiful outline, though I could see that it was Jewish too; and that, and all her features, were so fine that sculpture seemed a despicable art beside her; and certainly my pen is good for nothing. If any likeness of her could be given, it must be by sculpture, not painting. She was slender, and youthful, but yet had a stately and cold, though soft and womanly grace; and, looking at her, I saw what were the wives of the old patriarchs, in their maiden or early married days—what Rachel was, when Jacob wooed her seven years, and seven more—what Judith was; for womanly as she looked, I doubt not she could have slain a man, in a good cause—what Bathsheba was; only she seemed to have no sin in her—perhaps what Eve was, though one could hardly think her weak enough to eat the apple. I never should have thought of touching her; for, whether owing to distinctness of race, my sense that she was a Jewess, or whatever else, I felt a sort of repugnance, simultaneously with my perception that she was an admirable creature.[2]

In *The Marble Faun*, Miriam both paints and resembles the biblical Jewish women mentioned here. The description of her self-portrait (47–48), in fact, is a compressed and toned-down version of this passage. What is most striking about the original, though, is Hawthorne's fascinated and appalled sense of the unrepresentability of Emma Salomons. Again and again, the passage confesses its inability to describe either her features or her character. Moreover, she seems to Hawthorne a figure who somehow disables every medium of artistic representation—paint, stone, and language. So thoroughly do his conflicting feelings toward her unsettle the categories that order his response to experience that, as he observes her, the very blackness of black and the whiteness of white become uncertain and problematic propositions. Thus, the figure of the Jew, in the person of Emma Salomons, emblematizes the state of moral and epistemological chaos that both attracts and repels the characters and the narrator in *The Marble Faun*.

If Hawthorne projected the danger and allure of liberation from his own identity, of chaos, onto the young Jewish woman at the lord mayor's banquet, he projected onto her much older husband the terrifying force of fate. His notebook passage continues:

But, at the right hand of this miraculous Jewess, there sat the very Jew of Jews; the distilled essence of all the Jews that have been born since Jacob's time; he was Judas Iscariot; he was the Wandering Jew; he was the worst, and at the same time, the truest type of his race, and contained within himself, I have no doubt, every old prophet and every old clothesman, that ever the tribes produced; and he must have been circumcised as much [as] ten times over. I never beheld anything so ugly and disagreeable, and preposterous, and laughable, as the outline of his profile; it was so hideously Jewish, and so cruel, and so keen; and he had such an immense beard that you could see no trace of a mouth, until he opened it to speak, or to eat his dinner,—and then, indeed, you were aware of a cave, in this density of beard. And yet his manners and aspect, in spite of all, were those of a man of the world, and a gentleman. Well; it is as hard to give an idea of this ugly Jew, as of the beautiful Jewess. He was the Lord Mayor's brother, and an elderly man, though he looked in his prime, with his wig and dyed beard; and Rachel, or Judith, or whatever her name be, was his wife! I rejoiced exceedingly in this Shylock, this Iscariot; for the sight of him justified me in the repugnance I have always felt towards his race. (*Notebooks*, 321)

Much more plainly than the description of the young woman, this passage betrays Hawthorne's virulent anti-Semitism. We must not ignore the racism and anti-Semitism that Hawthorne shared with most white Christians of his time. But the point of quoting his essays, letters, and notebook entries about blacks and Jews is not to indulge in fruitless moral condemnation of the prejudices of those long dead; in this instance, Hawthorne's image of Philip Salomons provides additional insight into the social grounds and implications of the theme of fatality or determinacy in *The Marble Faun*.

As the "type of his race," the lord mayor's brother is a model. Hawthorne's language, moreover, associates him and his "race" with eternal repetition, just as Miriam's model is a character who is reproduced again and again and is associated with a crime repeated from generation to generation. Like Miriam's model, too, the figure of the Jew is represented here as an almost inconceivable union of the sensual and the intellectual, the primitive and the urbane. Even his hidden, evil cave of a mouth anticipates the subterranean cave from which the model emerges to consume the lives of Hawthorne's young protagonists. In fact, as the "distilled essence" of the Wandering Jew, Philip

Salomons does directly anticipate Miriam's model. For the legend of the specter of the catacombs that is offered as an explanation of the model's appearance in *The Marble Faun* is simply a version of the Christian legend of the Wandering Jew—the figure who supposedly mocked or spurned the suffering Jesus, for which he was condemned to wander the face of the earth eternally without any hope of salvation.

The strange union of chaos and fate that we find in the atmosphere of *The Marble Faun* has one of its sources, then, in Hawthorne's strangely married dinner companions in London. In associating the figure of the Jew both with the unstable mixture of opposing qualities (Emma Salomons) and with inevitable repetition (Philip Salomons), Hawthorne—probably unconsciously—mirrored a central contradiction in nineteenth-century anti-Semitic myths of the origin and evolution of the Jews. The influential French racial theorist, Count Joseph Arthur de Gobineau, had determined that "the Semites were a white hybrid race bastardized by a mixture with blacks."[3] Other researchers, however, such as the American surgeon Josiah Clark Nott, found the Jews to exemplify an uncanny racial purity such that modern-day representatives bear "the same features which the Almighty shaped on the first pairs which he created," a phenomenon attributable in part to "the custom of 'sleeping with their fathers.'"[4] However much or little Hawthorne knew of such theories, it seems clear that, in a novel written at an ominous and insecure moment in his own life and in the history of his country, he drew on available stereotypes of the Jews and on his own images of Emma and Philip Salomons to find symbols and scapegoats for his mingled sense of disorientation and of doom.

As we have seen throughout this study, many cultural and personal circumstances shaped *The Marble Faun*. Gender roles, religious, sexual, and aesthetic values, nationalism, the professional identity of the artist, the autonomy of the individual, and the effects of the past on the present are all at issue in the novel. Hawthorne's apprehensions about the health crisis in his family, the political crisis in the United States, and his own crisis of vocation contributed as well to the feeling of existential homelessness that *The Marble Faun* conveys, as if Hawthorne and his representative Americans had become types of the Wandering Jew, permanent inhabitants of what, in the later passage about the uprooted slaves, he would call "the stranger's land." Of course, at the end of the novel, Hilda, Kenyon, and the narrator separate themselves from Miriam, Donatello, and the legacy of the murdered model. In the later chapters, too, Hawthorne abandons and finally denies outright the strong early suggestions of Miriam's Jewishness. But as one critic's topographical analysis shows, the movements of the characters in the last third of *The Marble Faun* take them back and forth across what was for Hawthorne the strangest quarter of the stranger's land—the area of Rome that in the 1850s was the Jewish ghetto (Goldman, 387). The partial repression of the racial theme in the novel finally is representative of Hawthorne's response to the many challenges that presented themselves in Europe to what, in the first chapter, I called the established principles of his identity. These challenges were posed by new stimuli, new circumstances, and new self-examination that, in the end, were too threatening to embrace. In simultaneously confronting and avoiding or repressing them, Hawthorne can be likened to his heroine Hilda, who dutifully takes the fallen Miriam's package to the Cenci palace, which sits in the midst of the "close, unclean, and multitudinous" ghetto (388), but who resists knowing what is going on around her: "she had trodden as if invisible," Hawthorne writes, "and not only so, but blind" (387).

8

Conclusion: *The Marble Faun* and the Reader

In a passage that we examined in chapter 5, Hawthorne describes Saint Peter's as a work of art that "can nowhere be made visible at one glance. It stands in its own way. You see an aisle or a transept; you see the nave, or the tribune; but, on account of its ponderous piers and other obstructions, it is only by this fragmentary process that you get an idea of the Cathedral" (349). This is an apt characterization of *The Marble Faun* itself and of the problem of reading it. The novel often seems so crowded with significant details, symbols, and events, so choked with ponderous meanings, that one has little room for interpretive maneuvering and little chance of giving these materials a coherent shape. Not only does the novel offer too much; it also seems to offer too little. Crucial information and explanations are withheld; dramatic and revelatory scenes (the hours that Miriam and Donatello pass together after the model's death, Hilda's interview at the Cenci palace and her subsequent detainment) are unwritten. The reader must supply the connections, must fill in the gaps with material provided by his or her own imagination, judgment, or desire.

The reader's role, like that of the viewer of Saint Peter's, is at once a creative and a repressive one. Both works, the novel and the church, are impossible to perceive in their entirety; their parts can be observed, but their overall design is apprehended as an idea, an image, a creative construct. And for the viewer or the reader to project a comprehensive design, a certain amount of repression is required—that is, any unified view or interpretation must deny the self-obstructions of these works and the sense of fragmentedness and uncertainty that is part of the experience of encountering them. *The Marble Faun* abounds in acts of viewing, analyzing, and judging, and we might well argue that the problem of *reading,* broadly construed, is as much the novel's subject as are the other matters—the Fall, the powers and limits of art, religion, nationality, writing and sexual identity, the psychology of race, the existential condition of the self—that have occupied us in previous chapters. Hawthorne's narrative in fact contains notable examples of both the creative and the repressive operations of reading that its readers necessarily perform.

In the chapter entitled "Fragmentary Sentences," Hawthorne's narrator prefaces his account of the only conversation between Miriam and the model that the novel presents by disclaiming accurate or complete knowledge of that event. Putting himself in the position of a reader or receiver of information, he explains:

> There have come to us but a few vague whisperings of what passed in Miriam's interview, that afternoon, with the sinister personage who had dogged her footsteps ever since the visit to the catacomb. In weaving these mystic utterances into a continuous scene, we undertake a task resembling, in its perplexity, that of gathering up and piecing together the fragments of a letter, which has been torn and scattered to the winds. Many words of deep significance—many entire sentences, and those possibly the most important ones—have flown too far, on the winged breeze, to be recovered. If we insert our own conjectural amendments, we perhaps give a purport utterly at variance with the true one. Yet, unless we attempt something in this way, there must remain an unsightly gap, and a lack of continuousness and dependence in our narrative. (93)

Even without portions of the narrative literally missing, the sentences of *The Marble Faun* remain fragmentary, the gaps between them and the interpretive spaces within them calling forth the kind of creative participation on the part of the reader that the narrator models here.

The reader's repressive operation is modeled by Hilda, who is herself a kind of reader or critic—an expert consumer and transmitter of images, and an elucidator of meanings, produced by others. Hilda is characterized as a perfect copyist, but Hawthorne stipulates that she achieves her brilliant effect not by re-creating every material detail of her original but by selectively ignoring them or subtly abstracting from them:

> It was not Hilda's general practice to attempt reproducing the whole of a great picture, but to select some high, noble, and delicate portion of it, in which the spirit and essence of the picture culminated. . . . The copy would come from her hands with what the beholder felt must be the light which the Old Master had left upon the original in bestowing his final and most ethereal touch. In some instances, even, (at least, so those believed, who best appreciated Hilda's power and sensibility,) she had been enabled to execute what the great Master had conceived in his imagination, but had not so perfectly succeeded in putting upon canvas. (58–59)

Hilda's copies, in other words, are interpretations that seek to evoke their originals' most sublime idea (their "spirit" and "essence") by omitting or repressing everything that could obstruct or fragment it. When we examine this passage, we recognize how Hilda's exclusive focus on the "final" or "culminat[ing]" truth of a work of art eliminates all traces of mixed intention, struggle, or *process* that the original might contain; it even may subordinate the actual *product* itself, as in the case of the originals that do not even in part match Hilda's conception but only seem to have aspired toward what "she had been enabled to execute." Hilda, then, does what readers of "power and sensibility" typically do and what all readers, to some extent, must do: she makes sense by rationalizing or idealizing her object, by re-creating an imperfect artifact—embedded in and affected by history—as an ethereal image.

The readings of *The Marble Faun* that I have offered in the preceding chapters complement one another in various ways but perhaps complicate and even obstruct one another more. No one of them can fully incorporate the rest. This is not simply because they draw on different evidence from the text or address themselves to different aspects of it. It is also because these readings are the results of different critical approaches, different kinds of critical attention. Literary works are brought into being through the interaction of an author, a language, and the world to which author and language have reference, and they only continue to exist through the interpretive reproductions of that interaction that readers perform. As readers, we—like Hilda—bring to our task certain principles, values, and techniques that enable us to enter into the particular interaction of author, language, and world that is our text but that necessarily affect that interaction in some way. Our reproductions bring to light some portion of the original or shine a light that gives prominence to some pattern; but every illumination casts a shadow, and every pattern that emerges obscures a possible alternative. In this book, I have not pretended that *The Marble Faun* could be brought into "broad and simple daylight," or that any one reading could be so sufficient as to have "no shadow." Rather, I have tried to hold the novel up to different critical lights.

The chapter 4 discussion of Hawthorne's use of the theme of the Fall reflects several conventional critical assumptions. It assumes that what is important about the novel is some central propositional statement that it may make: "The Fall should (or should not) be understood to have been fortunate." Further, it assumes that the author, Hawthorne, is in full control of the ideas and the language involved in formulating and articulating the proposition. This critical approach takes the primary materials of the novel to be the biblical myths and historical archetypes upon which Hawthorne conspicuously drew. Its general orientation is humanistic in that it implicitly understands a work of literature to be an individual's creative effort to affirm some meaning—in this case, the moral significance of human existence itself.

The opening pages of chapter 5 move from the generative myths of Western culture to the historical circumstances that provided American Protestants of Hawthorne's time and place with certain attitudes toward and images of Catholicism. After briefly establishing this context for Hawthorne's treatment of his characters' and his own "Catholic propensities," however, the chapter focuses on the juxtapositions of opposing religious and aesthetic values within the text itself. For this reason, its general orientation may be termed formalist. More than any of the other three chapters that offer readings of *The Marble Faun*, chapter 5 restricts itself to the analysis of textual patterns and structures and to the evaluation of their degree of synthesis or polarization. It casts its critical light, we might say, not so much on what the author says as on what the work does. While this approach tends to present the work as illustrating a problem or a tension—rather than the author as stating an answer—it continues to grant intentional authority to the author through the work; it assumes, in other words, that the novel's more or less overt and conscious concerns define what it is about.

Chapter 6 represents a significant departure from the approaches and assumptions of the two previous chapters. Incorporating the principles and values of some of the more recent critical methodologies, it reads *The Marble Faun* in the light of historicist, psychological, and especially feminist analysis. In this view, Hawthorne's novel may appear to us to share the character of Miriam's compulsive paintings of biblical murderesses, paintings that she deems "not things that I created, but things that haunt me." It is, like Miriam's work, the product of certain complex personal relations to gender roles that are deeply engrained in and powerfully enforced by the larger society. *The Marble Faun* is most interesting, from this standpoint, not as a vehicle of humane wisdom, nor as an object in and of itself, but as an accessible and vivid site of Hawthorne's lifelong struggle, and of the struggle of American culture at an important moment in its development, with the psychology and politics of gender.

In chapter 7 the authority of the author and the centrality of the literary object are further eroded as the relative power of language and of the world increase. Drawing on insights associated with the critical theory known as deconstruction (which understands language to be a system of relationships between terms that do not have essential, autonomous meanings but only relative, and therefore unstable, ones), this chapter emphasizes the constant transformations of the meanings of words and images and even of the identities of characters in *The Marble Faun*. The chapter goes on to historicize this chaos by connecting it with the general destabilization of traditional understandings of the self that was brought about by new social and economic conditions in mid-nineteenth-century America and with the political crisis over how racial identity was to be understood and racial relations organized in the United States. Proceeding along lines set out by practitioners of cultural criticism, or what has been called "the new historicism," this last reading is more concerned with what the novel represses than what it acknowledges or affirms. It seeks to expose the stamp of the culture's dominant ideology upon the text and the covert and even unconscious ways in which the text passes it on.

All of these readings offer a literary work that is generated by the interaction of author, language, and world, but each defines and arranges these terms differently and accords them different amounts and kinds of power. The status of the author, for instance, changes drastically as we move from the first reading to the last. Hawthorne, the authoritative master of literary archetypes and free explorer of the mysteries of human experience, becomes a subject of psychological forces and culturally determined patterns of behavior and belief that he does not control and of which he may not even be aware. Interestingly, the different statuses of the author in the readings of *The Marble Faun* presented here raise one of the questions that we have seen the novel raise as well: Is the individual subject bound or free? Is identity determined or, at the other extreme, infinitely mutable, incoherent, unmoored? In light of our multiple interpretations, we may raise a similar question about our own activity as readers. Can we put forward a reading that enacts our critical freedom and power as it coherently interprets and identifies the novel for us? Or does each of our various critical methods (or models) mechanically yield the arbitrary meaning that it is predisposed to produce, leaving us with a chaotic array of incompatible fragments?

The answer I would give also suggests the reason I organized this book as I have done. It is the answer that Emerson gives on the first page of his volume of essays *The Conduct of Life*, published in 1860, the year *The Marble Faun* appeared. Emerson's subject is the study of one's own time; he identifies the historical moment of his own writing as one in which people seem overwhelmed both by the idea of fate and by a sense of confusion, a sense that they are "incompetent to solve the times." His advice, though, seems to me to apply to the study of literature as well:

> If we must accept Fate, we are not less compelled to affirm liberty, the significance of the individual, the grandeur of duty, the power of character. This is true, and that other is true. But our geometry cannot span these extreme points, and reconcile them. What to do? By obeying each thought frankly, by harping, or, if you will, pounding on each string, we learn at last its power. By the same obedience to other thoughts, we learn theirs, and then comes some reasonable hope of harmonizing them. . . . If one would study his own time, it must be by this method of taking up in turn each of the leading topics which belong to our scheme of human life, and, by firmly stating all that is agreeable to experience on one, and doing the same justice to the opposing facts in the others, the true limitations will appear. (Emerson, 943–44)

Every idea, every reading, has its particular power and particular limitations. In pursuing disparate thoughts, disparate approaches, as far as they will take us, we may never reach a point at which they resolve themselves into harmony. Ultimately, we may still be forced to choose between them. But it will be a true and meaningful choice because, knowing what it entails and what it excludes, we will be obliged to explain it and obliged to see how it explains us.

NOTES AND REFERENCES

1. Historical Context

1. D. H. Lawrence, "Nathaniel Hawthorne and *The Scarlet Letter*," in *A Casebook on the Hawthorne Question*, ed. Agnes McNeill Donohue (New York: Thomas Y. Crowell, 1963), 284.

2. Henry Wadsworth Longfellow, "[Review of] *Twice-Told Tales*," in *The Recognition of Nathaniel Hawthorne*, ed. B. Bernard Cohen (Ann Arbor: University of Michigan Press, 1969), 10; the essays collected in this volume are hereafter cited in the text as Cohen, followed by the page number.

3. Christopher Lasch, *Haven in a Heartless World* (New York: Basic Books, 1977).

4. Benjamin Franklin, *The Autobiography and Other Writings* (New York: Signet, 1961), 192.

5. Nathaniel Hawthorne, *The Centenary Edition of the Works of Nathaniel Hawthorne*, 20 vols., William Charvat, Roy Harvey Pearce, and Claude M. Simpson, general editors (Columbus: Ohio State University Press, 1962–), 1:10; this edition is hereafter cited in the text as *CE*, followed by the volume and page number.

6. Ralph Waldo Emerson, *Essays and Lectures* (New York: Library of America, 1983), 60; hereafter cited in the text as Emerson, followed by the page number.

2. The Importance of *The Marble Faun*

1. Hawthorne had great difficulty deciding on a title for *The Marble Faun* and sent lists of possible titles to both his English and his American publishers. His English publisher, Smith & Elder, decided on *Transformation*, a title that Hawthorne had once suggested but had come to dislike as "very flat and inexpressive" (*CE*, 4:xxvii). His American publisher, Ticknor &

Fields, accepted Hawthorne's preferred title, *The Marble Faun*. The American edition appeared one week after the English edition; both bore the subtitle "The Romance of Monte Beni," and except for the title, they were textually identical.

2. F. O. Matthiessen, *The American Renaissance* (New York: Oxford University Press, 1941), 352; Rudolph von Abele, *The Death of the Artist: A Study of Hawthorne's Disintegration* (The Hague: Martinus Nijhoff, 1955), 87.

3. Henry James, *Hawthorne* (London: Macmillan, 1879, Ithaca: Cornell University Press, 1966), 134; hereafter cited in the text as James, followed by the page number.

3. Critical Transformations

1. Henry James, *The Art of the Novel* (New York: Charles Scribner's Sons, 1962), 33.

2. Newton Arvin, *Hawthorne* (Boston: Little, Brown, 1929), 256.

3. Reprinted in Roy Harvey Pearce, *Historicism Once More* (Princeton: Princeton University Press, 1969), 175; hereafter cited in the text as Pearce 1969, followed by the page number.

4. Mark van Doren, *Nathaniel Hawthorne* (New York: Viking Press, 1957), 229.

5. Harry Levin, "Statues from Italy: *The Marble Faun*," in *Hawthorne Centenary Essays*, ed. Roy Harvey Pearce (Columbus: Ohio State University Press, 1964), 140; hereafter cited in the text as Pearce 1964, followed by the page number.

6. Leon Chai, *The Romantic Foundations of the American Renaissance* (Ithaca: Cornell University Press, 1987), 223.

7. Myra Jehlen, *American Incarnation: The Individual, the Nation, and the Continent* (Cambridge: Harvard University Press, 1986), 179–84.

8. Conrad Shumaker, "Daughter of the Puritans: History in Hawthorne's *The Marble Faun*," *New England Quarterly* 57, no. 1, (1984):83.

9. John Michael, "History and Romance, Sympathy and Uncertainty: The Moral of the Stones in Hawthorne's *Marble Faun*," *PMLA* 103 (March 1988):150–61.

10. Paul A. Lister, "Some New Light on Hawthorne's *The Marble Faun*," *Nathaniel Hawthorne Journal* 8, (1978):79–86.

11. Arnold Goldman, "The Plot of Hawthorne's *The Marble Faun*," *Journal of American Studies* 18 (December 1984):402; hereafter cited in the text as Goldman, followed by the page number.

12. Graham Clarke, "To Transform and Transfigure: The Aesthetic Play

of Hawthorne's *The Marble Faun*," in *Nathaniel Hawthorne: New Critical Essays*, ed. Robert A. Lee (London: Vision Press, 1982), 132.

13. John P. McWilliams, Jr., *Hawthorne, Melville, and the American Character* (Cambridge: Cambridge University Press, 1984), 126.

14. David B. Kesterson, "*The Marble Faun* as Transformation of Author and Age," *Nathaniel Hawthorne Journal* 8, (1978):70.

15. David Howard, "The Fortunate Fall and Hawthorne's *The Marble Faun*," in *Romantic Mythologies*, ed. Angus Fletcher (New York: Barnes and Noble, 1967), 103.

16. Henry S. Sussman, *High Resolution* (New York: Oxford University Press, 1989), 65.

4. The Fall of Man

1. Gordon Hutner, *Secrets and Sympathy: Forms of Disclosure in Hawthorne's Novels* (Athens: University of Georgia Press, 1988), 150.

2. Richard Harter Fogle, *Hawthorne's Fiction: The Light and the Dark* (Norman: University of Oklahoma Press, 1952), 191.

3. Richard H. Brodhead, *The School of Hawthorne* (New York: Oxford University Press, 1986), 77; hereafter cited in the text as Brodhead, followed by the page number.

4. George Edward Woodberry, *Nathaniel Hawthorne: How to Know Him* (Indianapolis: Bobbs-Merrill, 1918), 182.

5. Catholic Propensities

1. Quoted in Darrel Abel, *The Moral Picturesque: Studies in Hawthorne's Fiction* (West Lafayette, Ind.: Purdue University Press, 1988), 298.

2. Robert S. Levine, *Conspiracy and Romance: Studies in Brockden Brown, Cooper, Hawthorne, and Melville* (Cambridge: Cambridge University Press, 1989), 107, 106; hereafter cited in the text as Levine, followed by the page number.

3. Sigmund Freud, "The 'Uncanny,'" in *The Complete Psychological Works of Sigmund Freud*, 24 vols., tr. and ed. James Strachey, et al. (London: Hogarth Press, 1917–19), 17:226; hereafter cited in the text as Freud, followed by the page number.

4. Paul A. Lister, "Some New Light on Hawthorne's *The Marble Faun*," *Nathaniel Hawthorne Journal* 8, (1978):79.

6. The Rise of Women

1. Luther S. Luedtke, *Nathaniel Hawthorne and the Romance of the Orient* (Bloomington: Indiana University Press, 1989), x; hereafter cited in the text as Luedtke, followed by the page number.

2. Carroll Smith-Rosenberg, *Disorderly Conduct: Visions of Gender in Victorian America* (Oxford: Oxford University Press, 1986), 183; hereafter cited in the text as Smith-Rosenberg, followed by the page number.

3. Nathaniel Hawthorne, "Mrs. Hutchinson," in *The Works of Nathaniel Hawthorne*, 15 vols., ed. George Parsons Lathrop (Boston: Houghton Mifflin 1881–84), 12:218; hereafter cited in the text as *Works*, followed by the volume and page number.

4. Nina Baym, "Thwarted Nature: Nathaniel Hawthorne as Feminist," in *American Novelists Revisited: Essays in Feminist Criticism*, ed. Fritz Fleischmann (Boston: G. K. Hall, 1982), 60.

5. Quoted in Philip Young, *Hawthorne's Secret* (Boston: Godine, 1984), 6.

6. T. Walter Herbert, Jr., *Shamans of Domesticity: The Hawthornes and the Making of the Middle-Class Family* (Berkeley: University of California Press, 1992).

7. Gloria C. Erlich, *Family Themes and Hawthorne's Fiction: The Tenacious Web* (New Brunswick: Rutgers University Press, 1984), 118; hereafter cited in the text as Erlich, followed by the page number.

8. Quoted in Edward Wagenknecht, *Nathaniel Hawthorne: Man and Writer* (New York: Oxford University Press, 1961), 17.

9. Raymona E. Hull, "Una Hawthorne: A Biographical Sketch," *Nathaniel Hawthorne Journal* 6, (1976):94.

10. Louise K. Barnett, "American Novelists and the *Portrait of Beatrice Cenci*," *New England Quarterly* 53 (June 1980):173.

11. Sophia Hawthorne's complex response to her daughter's illness is brilliantly treated by Herbert in his chapter "Roman Fever," in which these remarks are quoted.

12. Carol Hanberry MacKay, "Hawthorne, Sophia, and Hilda as Copyists: Duplication and Transformation in *The Marble Faun*," *Browning Institute Studies* 12, (1984):93–120.

7. Fate, Chaos, and Repression

1. Quoted in Patrick Brancaccio, "Hawthorne's Miriam Identified," *Nathaniel Hawthorne Journal* 8, (1978):98.

2. Nathaniel Hawthorne, *The English Notebooks*, ed. Randall Stewart

Notes and References

(New York: Modern Language Association of America, 1941), 321; hereafter cited in the text as *Notebooks,* followed by the page number.

3. Robert Singerman, "The Jew as Racial Alien: The Genetic Component of American Anti-Semitism," *Anti-Semitism in American History,* ed. David A. Gerber (Urbana: University of Illinois Press, 1986), 104.

4. Josiah Clark Nott, "Physical History of the Jewish Race," *Southern Quarterly Review* 17, no. 3 (1850):431.

SELECTED BIBLIOGRAPHY

Primary Works

Twenty volumes of *The Centenary Edition of the Works of Nathaniel Hawthorne*, William Charvat, Roy Harvey Pearce, and Claude M. Simpson, general editors (Columbus: Ohio State University Press, 1962–) have appeared to date, including all the tales, romances, sketches, and children's writings, drafts of the late unfinished stories, the American, French, and Italian notebooks, and the letters. Still to be published are the English notebooks and miscellaneous writings.

Books

Fanshawe: A Tale. Boston: Marsh & Capen, 1828.

Twice-Told Tales. Boston: American Stationers Co., 1837.

Grandfather's Chair. Boston: E. P. Peabody; New York: Wiley & Putnam, 1841.

Biographical Stories for Children. Boston: Tappan & Dennet, 1842.

Twice-Told Tales (expanded edition). Boston: James Munroe & Co., 1842.

Mosses from an Old Manse. New York: Wiley & Putnam, 1846.

The Scarlet Letter: A Romance. Boston: Ticknor, Reed & Fields, 1850.

The House of the Seven Gables. Boston: Ticknor, Reed & Fields, 1851.

True Stories from History and Biography. Boston: Ticknor, Reed & Fields, 1851.

The Snow Image, and Other Twice-Told Tales. Boston: Ticknor, Reed & Fields, 1852.

A Wonder-Book for Girls and Boys. Boston: Ticknor, Reed & Fields, 1852.

Selected Bibliography

The Blithedale Romance. Boston: Ticknor, Reed & Fields, 1852.
Life of Franklin Pierce. Boston: Ticknor, Reed & Fields, 1852.
Tanglewood Tales for Girls and Boys. Boston: Ticknor, Reed & Fields, 1853.
Mosses from an Old Manse (revised edition). Boston: Ticknor & Fields, 1854.
The Marble Faun, or The Romance of Monte Beni. Boston: Ticknor & Fields, 1860; *Transformation, or The Romance of Monte Beni.* London: Smith & Elder, 1860.
Our Old Home. Boston: Ticknor & Fields, 1863.

Secondary Works

Biographical and Critical Studies: Books

Anderson, Quentin. *The Imperial Self.* New York: Alfred A. Knopf, 1971. Opposes Hawthorne to tradition of Emerson, Whitman, and James in the value he places on society and the limitations he places on the self.

Arvin, Newton. *Hawthorne.* Boston: Little, Brown, 1929. A biographical study focusing on Hawthorne's alienation.

Baym, Nina. *The Shape of Hawthorne's Career.* Ithaca: Cornell University Press, 1976. Hawthorne's works considered in chronological order, tracing his professional development.

Brodhead, Richard H. *The School of Hawthorne.* New York: Oxford University Press, 1986. Examines Hawthorne's legacy and the importance of his image for later American writers and contains a fine chapter on *The Marble Faun.*

Carton, Evan. *The Rhetoric of American Romance: Dialectic and Identity in Emerson, Dickinson, Poe, and Hawthorne.* Baltimore: Johns Hopkins University Press, 1985. Reads Hawthorne's novels in the context of nineteenth-century American "romance," defined as a form of literary engagement with questions about the relation of words to things and the nature of the self.

Cohen, B. Bernard, ed. *The Recognition of Nathaniel Hawthorne: Selected Criticism since 1828.* Ann Arbor: University of Michigan Press, 1969. A collection of important reviews and criticism over the years.

Crews, Frederick C. *The Sins of the Fathers: Hawthorne's Psychological Themes.* New York: Oxford University Press, 1966. A Freudian interpretation of Hawthorne's works.

Dryden, Edgar A. *Nathaniel Hawthorne: The Poetics of Enchantment.* Ithaca: Cornell University Press, 1977. Explores the motifs of enchantment and disenchantment in attempting to locate the spirit of the author in Hawthorne's writings.

Erlich, Gloria C. *Family Themes and Hawthorne's Fiction: The Tenacious Web.* New Brunswick: Rutgers University Press, 1984. Study of themes of the family in Hawthorne's works as shaped by his growing up in the Manning household.

Fogle, Richard Harter. *Hawthorne's Fiction: The Light and the Dark.* Norman: University of Oklahoma Press, 1952, Rev. ed. 1964. The patterning of Hawthorne's imagery and symbolism is discussed to bring out his techniques and worldview.

Herbert, T. Walter, Jr. *Shamans of Domesticity: The Hawthornes and the Making of the Middle-Class Family.* Berkeley: University of California Press, 1992. A study of Hawthorne's writings and married life as they exemplify and contribute to the emergence of American domestic ideology.

Hutner, Gordon. *Secrets and Sympathy: Forms of Disclosure in Hawthorne's Novels.* Athens: University of Georgia Press, 1988. Discusses the interpretive, imaginative, and moral demands that Hawthorne's use of secrets makes on his characters and his readers.

James, Henry. *Hawthorne.* London: Macmillan, 1879; Ithaca: Cornell University Press, 1966. The first full-length study of Hawthorne treats him as the representative American writer with the characteristic strengths and weaknesses of his country, as James defines them.

Luedtke, Luther S. *Nathaniel Hawthorne and the Romance of the Orient.* Bloomington: Indiana University Press, 1989. Demonstrates the importance of Hawthorne's readings on the Orient and of the figure of the Orient in his fiction.

Martin, Terence. *Nathaniel Hawthorne* (revised edition). Boston: Twayne, 1983. Useful general introduction to Hawthorne's life and writings.

Matthiessen, F. O. *The American Renaissance.* New York: Oxford University Press, 1941. Examines Hawthorne's works as part of the flowering of a self-consciously national American literature in the 1850s that explored and sought to give appropriate literary expression to the idea of democracy.

Mellow, James R. *Nathaniel Hawthorne in His Times.* Boston: Houghton Mifflin, 1979. Biographical study that emphasizes Hawthorne's public life and social engagement.

Newberry, Frederick. *Hawthorne's Divided Loyalties: England and America in His Works.* Cranbury, N.J.: Associated University Presses, 1987. A study of the significance of England and Hawthorne's English roots in his works.

Von Abele, Rudolph. *The Death of the Artist: A Study of Hawthorne's Disintegration.* The Hague: Martinus Nijhoff, 1955. Argues that Hawthorne's writing was facilitated by an ability to balance psychic tensions that he could not sustain in his later years.

Wagenknecht, Edward. *Nathaniel Hawthorne: Man and Writer.* New York: Oxford University Press, 1961. A study of Hawthorne's character and personality based on his fiction, letters, and journal entries.

Waggoner, Hyatt H. *Hawthorne: A Critical Study.* Cambridge: Harvard University Press, 1955. Hawthorne as a Christian opposed to the optimism of his time.

Critical Studies: Articles

Auerbach, Jonathan. "Executing the Model: Painting, Sculpture, and Romance-Writing in Hawthorne's *The Marble Faun.*" *ELH: A Journal of English Literary History* 47, no. 1 (1980): 103–20. Explores Hawthorne's self-reflective consideration of the aesthetic and moral dimensions of romance.

Baym, Nina. "Thwarted Nature: Nathaniel Hawthorne as Feminist." In *American Novelists Revisited: Essays in Feminist Criticism,* ed. Fritz Fleischmann, 58–77. Boston: G. K. Hall, 1982. A feminist approach to Hawthorne's women characters and their relationships to men and authority.

Carton, Evan. "A Daughter of the Puritans and Her Old Master: Hawthorne, Una, and the Sexuality of Romance." In *Daughters and Fathers,* ed. Lynda E. Boose and Betty S. Flowers, 208–32. Baltimore: Johns Hopkins University Press, 1989. Examines Hawthorne's highly charged association of writing and femininity as it shapes his fiction and his relationship with his daughter Una.

Howard, David. "The Fortunate Fall and Hawthorne's *The Marble Faun.*" In *Romantic Mythologies,* ed. Angus Fletcher, 97–136. New York: Barnes and Noble, 1967. Discusses the terror of the "revolutionary condition" in Hawthorne's last novel.

Levine, Robert S. "'Antebellum Rome' in *The Marble Faun.*" *American Literary History* 2, no. 1 (1990): 19–38. Reads the novel in the context of the American and Italian political situations of the time and particularly in relation to American anti-Catholic discourse.

Michael, John. "History and Romance, Sympathy and Uncertainty: The Moral of the Stones in Hawthorne's *Marble Faun.*" *PMLA* 103 (March 1988): 150–61. Discusses the problems of history and interpretation in the novel.

INDEX

Index

residence, 6, 48; divided identity of, 3–5, 77–84, 89, 93–94; gender politics of, 6–7, 9, 69, 70–96, 126; problem titling *The Marble Faun*, 24, *43–44*; residence in Italy, 10–11, 14, 49, 71, 86, 110; use of notebooks in *The Marble Faun*, 15–16, 94, 117–18

NON-FICTION
"Chiefly About War Matters," 114–15
English Notebooks, The, 117–19
Life of Franklin Pierce, 110–11, 114
Our Old Home, 116

NOVELS
Blithedale Romance, The, 14, 17, 20, 35, 48–49, 71, 109
House of the Seven Gables, The, 14, 20, 21
Scarlet Letter, The, 3, 8, 9, 20, 35, 43, 65, 71, 76–78, 109

TALES AND STORY COLLECTIONS
"Birthmark, The," 35
"Endicott and the Red Cross," 47
"Fragments from the Journal of a Solitary Man," 116
"Gray Champion, The," 47
"Mr. Higginbotham's Catastrophe," 82
Mosses from an Old Manse, 4, 80
"My Kinsman, Major Molineux," 35
"Passages From a Relinquished Work," 81–82, 84
"Rappaccini's Daughter," 35
The Snow Image, 78
Twice-Told Tales, 4, 83
"Young Goodman Brown," 35

Hawthorne, Sophia Peabody, 6, 9, 80, 83, 93
Hawthorne, Una, 9, 11, 46, *84–87*, 88, 90, 93, 95, 96
Herbert, T. Walter, 79
Hewitt, Fr. A. F., 45
Howe, Julia Ward, 83
Hutner, Gordon, 37

Indeterminacy. *See* Determinacy and indeterminacy
Interpretation, problem of, 3, 13, 15, 17–24, 27–28, 37–44, 104, *122–128*

James, Henry, 14, 18–19, 21
Jews and Judaism, in *The Marble Faun*, 21, 42, 58–59, 113, 116–21; Hawthorne's experience of, 11, 116–20

Lasch, Christopher, 6
Lawrence, David Herbert, 3, 4, 51
Levin, Harry, 22
Levine, Robert S., 46–47
Longfellow, Henry Wadsworth, 4, 6
Lowell, James Russell, 18, 42, 80
Luedtke, Luther S., 70–72

Mackay, Carol Hanberry, 94
Manning, Robert, 9, 79, 81, 84
Matthiessen, F. O., 13
Melville, Herman, 4, 6

New Criticism, The, 21–23
Nott, Josiah Clark, 120

Painting and sculpture, contrasted in *The Marble Faun*, 42–43, 59–66, 126
Peabody, Elizabeth, 111
Pearce, Roy Harvey, 21
Pierce, Franklin, 10, 110

THE AUTHOR

Evan Carton is associate professor of English at the University of Texas at Austin, where he teaches courses in American literature, criticism, and culture. He is the author of *The Rhetoric of American Romance* and the coauthor with Gerald Graff of the section on "Criticism since 1940" of the forthcoming *Cambridge History of American Literature*. He has also published essays on the work of American writers from Emerson to Joseph Heller, John Irving, Joan Didion, and novelists of the Vietnam War.